OUTLAWS, SPIES, AND GANGSTERS

Chasing Notorious Criminals

BY **Laura Scandiffio**

ART BY **Gareth Williams**

annick press
toronto + new york + vancouver

© 2014 Laura Scandiffio (text)
© 2014 Gareth Williams (illustrations)
Edited by Linda Pruessen
Designed by Sheryl Shapiro

Annick Press Ltd.

We acknowledge the support of the Canada Council for the Arts, the Ontario Arts Council, and the Government of Canada through the Canada Book Fund (CBF) for our publishing activities.

ONTARIO ARTS COUNCIL
CONSEIL DES ARTS DE L'ONTARIO
50 YEARS OF ONTARIO GOVERNMENT SUPPORT OF THE ARTS
50 ANS DE SOUTIEN DU GOUVERNEMENT DE L'ONTARIO AUX ARTS

Cataloging in Publication

Scandiffio, Laura, author
    Outlaws, spies, and gangsters : chasing notorious criminals / Laura Scandiffio ; art by Gareth Williams.

Includes bibliographical references and index.
ISBN 978-1-55451-621-6 (bound).—ISBN 978-1-55451-620-9 (pbk.)

    1. Criminals—Juvenile literature. 2. Criminals—Biography—Juvenile literature. I. Williams, Gareth Glyn, illustrator II. Title.

HV6027.S33 2014   j364.3092'2   C2013-906698-5

Distributed in Canada by:
Firefly Books Ltd.
50 Staples Avenue, Unit 1
Richmond Hill, ON L4B 0A7

Published in the U.S.A. by Annick Press (U.S.) Ltd.
Distributed in the U.S.A. by:
Firefly Books (U.S.) Inc.
P.O. Box 1338
Ellicott Station
Buffalo, NY 14205

Printed in China

Visit us at: www.annickpress.com
Gareth Williams is represented by Sparx Illustrators: www.africanillustrators.com

Also available in e-book format. Please visit www.annickpress.com/ebooks.html for more details. Or scan

To Rob
—L.S.

To Rene, Mom,
Dad, Warren,
and Ma Ansie
G.W.

IMAGE CREDITS
Fingerprint used throughout, © Openko Dmytro/Dreamstime.com; file folder used throughout, © iStockphoto Inc./Roel Smart; handcuffs and gun used throughout, © Ivan Gusev/Dreamstime.com; rubber stamps used throughout, © Ints Vikmanis/Dreamstime.com

TABLE OF CONTENTS

ON THE TRAIL OF A CRIMINAL

When two officers knocked on the door of a lonely cabin in the wilderness, they had no idea of the long, dangerous ordeal ahead. There was no warning that inside crouched a desperate fugitive who was about to lead them on a chase that would become a life-and-death struggle. As the manhunt for Albert Johnson would prove, capturing a suspect can turn into a fierce quest: a battle of wits and stamina between a fugitive from justice and the searchers in pursuit.

The stories in this book are accounts of those hunts and captures—eight dramatic chases that unfolded around the world, from the 1930s to the present day. From an arctic manhunt on dogsled and snowshoe, to tracking the electronic trail of a cybercriminal, each of these hunts pits a very different kind of suspect against a range of pursuers. A bank robber on a destructive road trip with federal agents on his trail; a long-vanished war criminal living under another name but tracked down at last by secret agents; a spy hiding in plain sight among the CIA agents he is betraying. From gangsters to dictators and terrorists, fugitives from the law have been chased by police, intelligence agents, and the military, including special operations forces such as Navy SEALs or Rangers. The hunt might span a country, or the world. It might last hours, weeks, or years.

Each chase is unique, with law enforcement trying new techniques or technology and learning painful lessons from mistakes. The Federal Bureau of Investigation (FBI) was still in its early days when its agents hunted "Public Enemy" John Dillinger, and the agency learned from its blunders, changing the way it conducted searches and communicated with police. The FBI that went after the spy Aldrich Ames or the cyber thief Vladimir Levin was a much more effective and experienced force.

While it's usually the police who hunt suspected criminals,

sometimes the pursuit is taken on by the military, as in the case of major terrorists or leaders who have committed international crimes. These hunts can be controversial, and risk causing conflict between nations. Chasing the dictator and drug trafficker Manuel Noriega involved a military invasion of another country, Panama, by U.S. forces. The hunt for terrorist Osama bin Laden also resulted in the American military taking action on foreign soil, this time in secret.

Sometimes the approach of pursuers is loud and clear—the hunt is widely publicized, and police ask the public for help by circulating photos and information on the suspect, or even enlist the help of police forces in other countries. The Citibank cyber robbery could not have been solved without this kind of international cooperation. This strategy can also make a fugitive feel there is nowhere left to hide, and may even pressure a suspect to surrender—tactics like this were used to corner the Jamaican gangster Christopher Coke. Other times the last thing the searchers want is for the suspect to know they are coming, and the hunt is carried out in secret. Adolf Eichmann, a notorious Nazi war criminal, had slipped through the nets of searchers before and hidden his identity for 12 years. The undercover Israeli agents tracking him in Argentina knew that one false move could tip off their suspicious quarry, and he would slip away again, perhaps forever.

When a whole team pursues one fugitive it might seem the pursuers have the advantage, but sometimes it's like searching for a needle in a haystack. And some fugitives may have sources of power that are hard to match—wealth, armed allies, a safe haven. Occasionally, a fugitive becomes a sympathetic figure to the public— seen as an underdog or a rebel. For many poor people during the Depression, the bank robber John Dillinger seemed like a modern-day Robin Hood. Many Jamaicans living in the community dominated by Christopher Coke felt they owed him a debt of loyalty, despite his many crimes. These cases are exceptions, though. In contrast, General Manuel Noriega was so detested in Panama that he was kept on the run, and his American pursuers got vital information from his many enemies.

These eight stories also show how much hunts for criminals have changed over time. During the 1931–32 pursuit of the "Mad Trapper" by Mounties across the Northwest Territories, radio and aircraft were two new crime-fighting innovations used for one of the first times. But the search's success or failure would depend most of all upon the wits and strength of those on the ground, tracking prints and telltale clues in the landscape, and putting their survival skills to the test. By the time of the hunt for Osama bin Laden, over 70 years later, much had changed. Drones flying overhead could film faraway terrain, sending images back to searchers in real time. Thermal imaging deployed from helicopters mapped the presence of humans hidden in buildings on the ground. Stealth technology allowed aircraft to pursue a target in deadly silence. But high-tech search methods do not guarantee a capture, as fugitives have found ways to foil technology—Osama bin Laden ducked American tracking efforts for years by giving up cell phones and the Internet, and counting on human beings to act as his messengers. In the end, however, it was one of these human contacts that led searchers to a breakthrough. Many investigators insist that what still matters most in a hunt is "good human intelligence"—reliable tips from people. No amount of gadgets can make up for a lack of solid leads. In the end, human ingenuity will prove more crucial than technology. And while luck may play a role in any chase, a successful capture will depend most of all on the courage and perseverance of the searchers.

THE MAD TRAPPER: MANHUNT IN THE NORTH

NAME: known as Albert Johnson

BORN: unknown

WANTED FOR: harassing Native Canadian trappers, firing on RCMP officers, resisting arrest, and evading police

LOCATION OF CHASE: Northwest Territories and Yukon

DURATION: 54 days (December 26, 1931–February 17, 1932)

LAW ENFORCEMENT INVOLVED: Royal Canadian Mounted Police, Royal Canadian Signal Corps, Special Constables, and Native Canadian guides

Northwest Territories, Canada, 1931

A fierce north wind bit the Mountie's face as his sled hurtled across the frozen terrain, pulled by a team of barking dogs straining at the end of taut lines. Constable Alfred King drove in the lead, breaking trail, while his partner, Joe Bernard, followed with his own dog team. Both were young men in their early twenties. This wasn't how King had expected to spend the day after Christmas, but in a way he relished it. When he had joined the Royal Canadian Mounted Police (RCMP), he had volunteered for northern service. Patrols by dogsled and isolated posts in the rugged Yukon had made him tough. No one in the force had beaten him yet at a wrestling match!

The officer in charge of the Arctic Red River detachment, Constable Edgar Millen, had sent King and Bernard to check in on a newcomer to the North. On Christmas Day, a Native Canadian trapper from Rat River had trekked to Millen's RCMP post to complain: a white stranger was spoiling his traps, springing them and tossing them into the trees. This was serious—trappers depended on the animals they caught for survival, to feed their families and to make a living selling the pelts. The trapper believed the stranger's name was Albert Johnson.

Millen had recognized that name. He'd met a man known as Johnson last summer at a general store buying supplies. Born in Ireland, Edgar "Spike" Millen had been a Mountie in the Canadian north for over seven years. He was well liked and got along with the locals. Like all Mounties, he took an interest in newcomers and asked them routine questions, mostly to discover if they were up to survival in the North. After all, it was men like Millen who would end up rescuing a hapless trapper who couldn't take care of himself.

Johnson had arrived by river on a homemade raft and spent the summer stocking up on supplies in the small settlements—paying with cash out of a can and saying very little to curious shopkeepers.

To the Mountie, he gave vague answers and avoided revealing anything about himself. Millen remembered him as about average height, strongly built, with light blue eyes. He thought he recalled hearing a trace of a Scandinavian accent in the stranger's voice. That same summer, men at a fishing camp saw Johnson drive a pair of long sticks into a riverbank, then stand back. Holding a pistol in each hand, he shot off the tops of the sticks, then crossed arms and did it again. Was the display meant to intimidate those watching? The men weren't sure, but they stayed away.

Now King and Bernard were on a journey to Johnson's log cabin. Word was that he'd built it himself after paddling up Rat River in a canoe he'd bought. It was also said that a couple of Native trappers who had knocked on his door expecting a customary mug of tea had instead faced a silent man who warned them away with his rifle. King didn't want any trouble. He would tell Johnson to leave others' traplines alone, and remind him to buy a trapping license.

The trip to Johnson's cabin had its own dangers. Dogsleds were the fastest means of travel in the North at that time—and still it would be a grueling two-day trek. With temperatures between −30 and −50 degrees Celsius (−22 and −58 degrees Fahrenheit), winter days above the Arctic Circle afforded only a few hours of dim light before darkness overtook travelers. Routes for dogsleds followed frozen rivers—icy paths that could sometimes give way or cause sleds to sink into traps of slush. Both men knew the dangers of getting wet here. Unless they could start a fire quickly to dry themselves—a difficult task in extreme cold—a soaking could turn fatal.

The morning of December 28, King and Bernard sighted the cabin. Built with spruce logs, it was the size of a single small room. The lonely dwelling sat on a high point with a clear view from three of its sides, the curving banks of the Rat River enclosing it in a semi-circle. King spotted a pair of homemade willow snowshoes leaning on the outside wall, and smoke coming out of the stovepipe chimney. Johnson must be home.

"Hello!" King shouted, then walked up to the cabin door and knocked with his mittened hand.

"Mr. Johnson," he called through the closed door, "my name is Constable King. I've received a complaint about you interfering with traplines. I'd like to ask you a few questions."

No answer. King took a closer look at the small window next to the door, and started in surprise. A face stared back at him. Then the burlap sack that covered the window dropped and the face disappeared from view.

King and Bernard exchanged glances. Both were getting uneasy. It was strange in this wild region for anyone to ignore a knock at the door. An unwritten rule guaranteed help to travelers who stopped at anyone's cabin. Something was wrong.

Maybe they had alarmed Johnson. The Mountie spoke again through the shut door, emphasizing that he was there only to ask questions. Then King and Bernard waited, pacing to keep warm. A whole hour passed in eerie silence, the sound of their panting dogs the only noise.

"We'll need a warrant before we can do anything." King sighed. That meant another trek of over 120 kilometers (75 miles) to their divisional commander at Aklavik. There, Inspector Eames supplied the warrant, along with two more constables. The men still hoped a

MUSH!

Travel by dogsled in the North is often called "mushing." Standing at the back of a sled, a "musher" is pulled across the snow by a team of up to 10 or 12 harnessed dogs, usually huskies, whose thick coats help them survive the cold. The dogs are picked for their size, power, and stamina.

"Mush!" is also the command to drive the dogs forward. The word may come from the French verb "marcher" (to go or to walk), as the early French settlers and fur traders in Canada used dog teams to transport cargo and people across snow-covered terrain.

brief word with Johnson would resolve things. They sped through the return trip, nearing the cabin on December 31 around noon. If they hurried, everyone agreed, they might even make it to the New Year's Eve party at a local trader's cabin. No one guessed how quickly events would escalate—or how deadly a turn they would take.

At Johnson's cabin, smoke once again trailed upward from the chimney. And still there was no answer to their shouts.

Three of the men waited on the riverbank while King walked up to the door. This time he was more careful. Pressing himself up against the wall with no window, he stood alongside the door, stretched out his arm, and knocked.

Instantly, a gunshot exploded in the wintry stillness. King felt pain rip through his chest as he fell to the ground. The shot had been fired straight through the cabin's small wood door. Although dazed, instinct propelled King to crawl away, pulling himself across the snow, toward the riverbank. The other Mounties fired shots at the cabin to give their partner time to make it to safety. The man in the cabin was firing back, and a bullet narrowly missed one constable's head. Once King neared the river, the men tumbled down behind the cover of the riverbank, pulling King with them.

Johnson would have to wait. King was

LAW AND ORDER IN THE NORTH

In the 1930s, the Royal Canadian Mounted Police, known as Mounties, were spread thin in the Northwest Territories and Yukon. A cavalry force founded in 1873 as the North-West Mounted Police, they were to maintain law and order in the new Northwest Territories. A handful of constables were responsible for policing wide expanses of territory. Between the small settlements and trading posts, trappers worked in isolation much of the time. Arctic Red River had a police detachment of three men; Aklavik had 11 constables and a commander. Also at Aklavik was a detachment of the Royal Canadian Corps of Signals, a unit of the army responsible for radio communications in the North. Radio was still a new technology in its early years. The Signals' radio beacons guided mail planes. Two-way radio communication proved a lifeline to isolated northerners— and was to play an important role in the hunt for Johnson.

bleeding and unresponsive. It was a long way back to Aklavik, with weary dogs and blowing snow that would make the entire trek an exhausting battle against the wind. But it was a race now to save King's life. They plunged ahead, pausing only to rub King's face to prevent frostbite. Twenty hours later they carried King into the small hospital. The news was good: the shot had pierced his torso but come out on the other side, missing his heart and other organs. King was strong; that was their best hope.

Now the Mounties knew they were dealing with more than a hermit or recluse—this was a desperate man. Someone who was violently determined to be left alone, and not to be seen by the police. Who was he? And what was he hiding, or perhaps running from?

On January 4, a force of seven men, including Inspector Eames, set out once more from Aklavik, well equipped with 42 dogs. On the way they picked up Spike Millen—the only Mountie who had actually seen and talked to Johnson. The men also loaded dynamite onto their sleds. About 13 kilometers (8 miles) from the cabin they camped and talked strategy. Their main fear was an ambush by

Johnson, who surely would guess they were coming, and could hide in the brush in countless places along the river. They decided not to approach the same way as before. Instead, they would circle the cabin. Two scouts sent ahead reported that Johnson's chimney smoke was still visible. Eames wondered: Why hadn't he run?

At noon on January 9, Eames led the approach to the cabin. While they were still some distance away he shouted, "Constable King is alive!" Maybe if Johnson knew he was not wanted for murder, he would be less desperate.

Again, only silence. Eames nodded to his men, who strode toward the cabin. As soon as they were in range, shots rang out. Johnson was firing through loopholes he had pierced in the spruce-log walls. From the level of the shots, the men could tell he was either lying on the floor or had dug a pit in which to stand and fire. The posse retreated to the cover of the riverbank. Despite their numbers, Johnson had the

advantage. He was warm, protected by walls, and out of sight, while they lay exposed in freezing temperatures. The Mounties built fires and took turns warming up, then storming the cabin in an attempt to knock down its door. Each time, the men retreated under the barrage of Johnson's heavy fire. Hours passed without success, and darkness set in.

"Thaw the dynamite," Eames ordered. They would have to force the mysterious recluse out.

Weakened by the extreme cold, the blasts did little damage to the sturdy log cabin. It was the middle of the night when the Mounties lit the fuse on the last bundle of dynamite. Eames sprinted from the riverbank and hurled it across the snow onto the cabin roof, then flung himself back toward the bank. This time the roof tore away; walls began to cave in. Eames and one of the posse— local tracker Karl Gardlund—sped for the cabin in a bid to reach it before Johnson recovered from the shock.

Panting, they halted against the log wall. Gardlund tied a flashlight to the end of a stick. If he could shine it inside the cabin, Eames could dash across the doorway and catch Johnson momentarily spotlit and dazed in the glare of the light. Stretching his arm, Gardlund moved the beam in front of the door that now sagged open. But before Eames could move, a single gunshot knocked the flashlight from the stick. Johnson was clearly unfazed by the explosion.

The men once again retreated to the riverbank, as heavy snow began to fall. After a 15-hour siege, Johnson was as defiant as ever. "Set fire to the cabin. Smoke him out," someone suggested. Eames shook his head. He wanted to capture Johnson alive. But their supplies were spent. Now Eames cursed the time wasted circling the cabin! In this cold, the men and dogs could not survive long without a steady supply of food to keep their body temperatures from dropping. They had no choice but to go back to Aklavik.

A week passed before Millen and Gardlund mushed back to the ruined cabin. It was deserted. The canoe was still there, but nothing else was left to offer a clue about their adversary. The snowshoes were gone, but a steady snowfall had covered any tracks.

It was a manhunt they faced now. And given Johnson's head start, the amount of wilderness to be searched was vast. Eames made a call for volunteers over the radio. A new force was bolstered by fresh recruits: experienced trappers, and two men from the army's radio corps, the Royal Canadian Signals—Sergeant Earl Hersey, a former Olympic runner, and R. F. Riddell, an old-time expert on northern survival. Together they set out on January 16. Eleven men from the Gwich'in (then called Loucheux) Native people joined them. The Signals brought a two-way radio—a very new innovation in police work—so they could stay in touch with their base during the manhunt. Some of the old-time trackers grumbled skeptically: it was a cumbersome piece of equipment, occupying a whole dogsled and always in danger of toppling and being damaged on the trail.

Eames knew from the start that food supplies would be the crucial issue. More searchers and dogs meant more mouths to feed and body temperatures to maintain in the wilderness. A lack of food could turn to hypothermia in short order. The hunt would also be a race against time.

For days they searched the landscape around the cabin—a wilderness crisscrossed with streams, and dotted with brush and spruce. The heavy snowfall had continued—and now turned to a blizzard. At night they camped around fires, nibbled their way through their store of bacon and hardtack biscuits, and drank tea. Food began to run out, and not one clue had been found. Blowing snow erased all tracks. Eames called back many of the volunteers—a leaner group led by Millen could travel farther and longer. Surely if they could hold out for a few more days, another week at most, they would have him.

For now, Millen could only guess where Johnson was headed by putting himself in his place. If he were on the run, he'd stick close to a river to avoid getting lost in a snowstorm. And so Millen and his team kept following the Rat River. Finally, they stumbled upon their first clue: a cache of food suspended from a tree, out of the reach of roaming animals. Would Johnson return for it? They lay in ambush for hours, ice forming on their beards, but without luck.

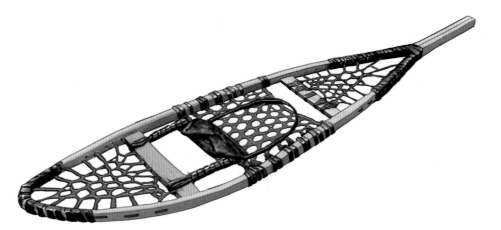

WANTED

The search was looking hopeless when one of the Signals spotted a snowshoe print on a patch of glassy ice. Its telltale shape matched the odd homemade ones seen outside Johnson's cabin. It was likely at least two days old, but the sight of the single print revitalized the group. At last!

Scanning the ice, they picked up a trail and began to follow it. Johnson was headed west, toward the Richardson Mountains. Frustratingly, they never seemed to catch up—the tracks were always old. Although no one but Millen had ever seen their quarry, the Mounties felt they were getting to know something of his mind by the clues left in his tracks. They became familiar with his tactics. Johnson traveled on packed snow, especially along riverbanks, so as to leave the scantest trail possible. His methods for eluding them were ingenious. The snowshoe tracks moved in continual zigzags, wasting the trackers' time and energy. It crossed Millen's mind that at any time, Johnson could be calmly watching them from a vantage point ahead on this crazy trail.

All of a sudden the tracks seemed to diverge, and the search party split up to follow both leads—only to run into each other when their trails met, hours later. They wasted precious time following a trail in the wrong direction before realizing Johnson must have put his snowshoes on backward to fool them. All the while they never spotted a fire or heard a gunshot in the distance. How was Johnson hiding his campfires—perhaps behind snowbanks? And he must be silently trapping small animals for food, to avoid making noise with his gun. It was almost beyond belief: how was this man outrunning their dogsleds on foot, carrying his supplies on his back, living off the land without leaving a trace? None of them had ever encountered anyone so expert at evasion and survival.

Pausing at the end of tracks that once again tapered off, Millen's men were startled to see a dog team approaching from a distance. On the sled was a Gwich'in trapper. He'd heard a gunshot near Bear River. Could Johnson have finally given in and shot some large prey for food? The chance was remote, but Millen decided to follow what looked like their only lead.

They passed the remains of a caribou carcass, and found what looked like a camp—but no one was there. The men combed the area on foot. Less than an hour later, Millen brought his team to a halt. He needed to think. Were they once again on a false trail? Then, a nearby sound made him catch his breath.

It was a man coughing.

No one spoke. They looked at one another, and nodded. Millen led his men slowly toward the direction of the sound. Again, they saw the familiar tracks, leading into trees. Through the trunks, down a bank at the bottom of a canyon, was Johnson, his back toward them. Beyond him was a steep cliff, cutting off any possible escape. He didn't even seem to know they were there.

They had an almost unbelievable advantage. Gardlund and Riddell began to inch their way down the bank. The way was steep, and they treaded carefully and silently. About 14 meters (15 yards) from Johnson's turned back, they crouched down and readied their weapons. Millen and another constable began quietly to follow them. Only a few steps down, one man's foot hit a patch of ice, and he slipped.

Johnson whirled around, lifted his rifle, and fired.

All four men dropped to the ground and returned fire. Johnson leaped across his campfire to dive behind a fallen tree. Gardlund fired at him as he arced into the air. Had he hit him? By the way Johnson seemed to crumple behind the large log, Gardlund guessed he had.

"Give yourself up!" Millen called.

No answer. Minutes passed, but felt much longer. Was Johnson even alive? No one wanted to approach the fallen tree.

The Mounties waited. Two hours passed with no sign of movement from behind the log. Soon it would be dark. Millen could stand the stalemate no longer. He rose and slowly made his way toward the log.

"Get down, Spike!" Riddell hissed, but Millen ignored him. Crouching, Riddell followed him. The other two men covered them with raised rifles.

"Watch it!" Riddell suddenly cried, and dove for cover. A rifle shot sounded.

Millen had just spotted Johnson's rifle barrel emerging over the log. He knelt down and fired back. Johnson's returning shots were rapid. Millen collapsed into the snow. Gardlund crawled on his stomach toward the fallen officer while the other two men fired toward Johnson to cover his move-ments. Under the volley of rifle shots, Gardlund tied Millen's bootlaces together to make a handle and pulled him to safety. But it was too late: Millen was already dead, shot in the heart. Further shots at Johnson's hiding place by the remaining three men were met with silence. Again he had slipped away.

Millen's death was a heavy blow to the searchers. Two men built a raised cache to protect their fallen comrade's body from predators while Riddell headed out by dogsled for Aklavik with the tragic news. Investigating Johnson's escape route, the remaining men saw he had mounted the sheer cliff of ice behind him, cutting footholds with an axe.

Upon hearing of the fatal shoot-out, Inspector Eames's deter-mination to find Johnson took on a grim resolve. Again he called upon volunteers. And he took a further, unprecedented step. He wanted a new ally in their manhunt: a pilot and aircraft to join the search. A plane had never been used before in Canadian crime fighting, but then the Mounted Police had never been so stumped by a fugitive. The government approved, and Wilfrid May, a World War I flying ace, and his trusted mechanic, Jack Bowen, took off in their monoplane to join the chase. May would search for Johnson from the sky, and rapidly supply the ground force with food that would take a week to bring by dogsled.

At first, bad luck continued to plague them. Blizzards covered tracks and kept grounding the plane, which had to be dug out of the snow. Yet their pursuit was drawing nearer to the Richardson Mountains, the northern tip of the Rockies along the Yukon border. Surely there was no way a man as exhausted as Johnson must be would try to cross them in winter! Then a hunter they met confirmed that his tracks had been seen on a mountain pass. The searchers were astounded. Who was this man they were chasing?

On Valentine's Day 1932, the weather cleared just long enough for May to fly westward to scan for signs of Johnson while the searchers below trudged on the ground. With a shout of joy, May spotted a line of snowshoe tracks. But he could spy no human figure.

Once over the mountains with May's help, the search party followed the winding Eagle River. Their flagging spirits rose when they found tracks less than a day old. News of the manhunt spread among the nearby Gwich'in people, and an elder told the Mounties not to go looking for him any more. "One sleep and he die," she said confidently.

On February 17, a day with little wind and no fog, the search party picked up its pace. In the lead, Sergeant Hersey's sled

rounded a sharp bend in the river. Ahead of him, about 280 meters (300 yards) away, was Johnson, backtracking on his own trail. The trapper had made a critical mistake. On the winding river, he had misjudged where his pursuers lay, thinking they were coming from the opposite direction.

Hersey grabbed his rifle and dropped to one knee. He called to Johnson to give himself up, and fired a shot. Johnson turned and ran, then suddenly twisted around and fired back. Hersey fell, badly injured.

As the other searchers raced to catch up, Johnson dashed out onto the frozen river. He dropped into the snow and took off his pack, using it as a shield. The searchers split into two groups, running alongside both banks of the river, flanking the fugitive. Calls for his surrender were met with defiant rifle shots. From the high ground of the riverbank, the men's shots hit Johnson in the side and shoulder. Despite obvious pain, he continued to fire back.

Seconds later, May soared overhead in his plane. Peering down at the river, he saw Johnson motionless in his trench of snow. May

PERSONAL EFFECTS OF ALBERT JOHNSON

The RCMP catalogued what they found on Johnson at the time of his death. Among his belongings they listed:

- Baking powder can containing $2,410 in cash (worth over $30,000 today)
- Small glass bottle containing five pearls and five pieces of gold dental work
- Small glass bottle containing gold dust and flakes (extracted by sifting gold-bearing gravel)
- Savage 30-30 rifle
- Iver Johnson sawed-off shotgun
- .22 Winchester rifle. Stock sawn off.
- Pocket compass
- Axe—handle bearing bullet mark
- Sack containing lard tin and lid used as tea pail, showing bullet holes
- Knife made from piece of metal, with moose-skin cover
- Moose-skin sewing pouch containing needles and thread
- Matches wrapped in tin foil
- Moose-skin folder containing mirror
- Gillette safety razor
- Handmade snowshoes

rocked his plane wings up and down in an attempt to signal that the fugitive was dead. Cautiously, the rest of the men climbed down the riverbanks and approached. Johnson was stretched out on his stomach. When they turned him over, the sight of his face sent a shock through each of them.

Johnson's lips were curled back, revealing his teeth in a terrible grimace—or was it a grin? To May, it looked like the face of a cornered creature who sees no way out and vows to bring down as many of his opponents as he can. The Mad Trapper had been defiant to the end. Both King and Hersey survived their wounds, but the Mounties were haunted by the image of Johnson's face, even years later.

The hunt was over, but the question remained: Who was he? Everyone knew him as Johnson, but there was no evidence that it was his real name. What did they know about him? Only that he had survived for seven weeks on the run in the Arctic, carrying a nearly 63-kilogram (138-pound) pack on his back. Obviously he was extraordinarily fit and strong. Had he been trained in the military? Where? What of the slight Scandinavian accent Millen remembered? None of the items found on him gave a clue to his identity. His clothes could have been bought at any general store by someone outfitting for the North. Among his belongings were gold and, surprisingly, pearls. This seemed like a tantalizing clue, but what did it mean?

When shopkeepers remembered how he had paid with so much cash stashed in a can, people surmised that he was an escaped bank robber, possibly a hardened lifelong criminal. Yet the doctor who examined his body found that he had excellent, expensive dental work—very advanced for the 1930s. At one time in his life, it seemed, he had been very well off. What was he doing in the North?

Apart from his eerie grimace, the man known as Albert Johnson had done nothing to enlighten his pursuers—throughout the entire saga, he never spoke a word.

The popular saying "The Mounties always get their man" seems to have spread at the time of the Mad Trapper's capture.

CAN FORENSICS SOLVE THE MYSTERY?

In 2007 a team of scientists unearthed the buried remains of the so-called Mad Trapper. Using modern forensic methods not available at the time of Johnson's death, they hoped to unlock the secret of his identity. With DNA samples from bone marrow, they were able to rule out the claims of many people who believed the fugitive was their long-lost relative. A study of teeth and nails can reveal clues about where a person spent much of his or her life, especially the early years, because things such as enamel are affected by local diet. In this way they concluded that the man came from either the United States or a Scandinavian country. His identity, however, remains a mystery.

JOHN DILLINGER: THE FIRST PUBLIC ENEMY NUMBER ONE

NAME: John Herbert Dillinger

BORN: June 22, 1903, in Chicago, Illinois

WANTED FOR: Armed robbery of banks and police arsenals; three jailbreaks; shoot-outs with police; leading a criminal gang that killed 10 people and wounded 7 others

LOCATION OF CHASE: Midwestern United States

DURATION: 10 months (September 1933–July 1934)

LAW ENFORCEMENT INVOLVED: Police in Indiana, Illinois, Arizona; FBI agents

Indiana, 1933

Just before three o'clock on a September afternoon, two neatly dressed men in suits and straw hats walked into the State Bank of Massachusetts Avenue in Indianapolis. The timing was no accident; cash deposits were at their peak for the day.

"This is a stick up!" one of the men shouted, handgun drawn. The other made an agile leap over the railing into the teller's cage. With his gun, he directed her to fill a sack with money. He did not seem in a hurry; in fact, he looked cool and calm.

Glancing up, the teller noticed a scar on his upper lip, and gray eyes that never left her. Lowering her gaze, she continued to pack in the bills with shaking hands. The man then emptied all the drawers of cash. "Open the vault," he demanded. An alarm sounded, but he continued to fill sacks with stacks of bills, tossing each full sack to his partner, who had his gun trained on the customers. Moments later, his accomplice directed the frightened customers into the vault and locked them in. The men were gone as suddenly as they had arrived, hopping into a waiting Chevrolet outside, and cruising—not too quickly—out of sight down the street.

It was a scene that had played out several times over the summer. A small gang of robbers was working its way through the banks of the Midwestern states. To catch the thieves, the banks' insurance company hired a private detective to follow a trail of clues that led from Michigan to Kentucky to Ohio. The Indiana State Police were also searching for the culprits, paying informants and staking out known haunts of criminals. Their hard work was about to pay off.

The newspapers would soon nickname the man who leaped over the tellers' railing "Jackrabbit." What did the police know about him? From what their snitches told them, they were pretty sure they were looking for a 29-year-old named John Dillinger. He'd been released from prison on parole in the spring, after serving nearly nine years for a bungled holdup in his hometown of Mooresville. The grocer he and his partner tried to rob knocked the gun from John's hand, and the two fled. John's hardworking father gave his son advice: confess and make a fresh start. He was sure the judge would go easy on him. To their shock, the judge made an example of John and sentenced him to 10 to 20 years.

John had been a reckless boy with a wild streak, always promising to straighten out when he got in trouble. But nine years in prison changed John Dillinger from a mischief-maker to something much more dangerous. Maybe those years had made him bitter, the police guessed, bitter enough to embark on a crime spree two months after getting out. Whether or not they were right, John Dillinger had certainly spent his life since the age of 20 among criminals in prison, learning the strategies of thieves. He was angry about his harsh sentence, and skeptical about getting a job with his criminal record. Most important, in prison he had met the men who would become his notorious gang.

Acting on tips from the private detectives, police arrested Dillinger within a month of the Indianapolis robbery, nabbing him as he tried to visit his girlfriend at her boarding house in Dayton,

THE GREAT DEPRESSION

When John Dillinger was released on parole in the spring of 1933, the country was in the grip of the Great Depression, a worldwide economic downturn that began in 1929 and lasted until about 1939. Across the United States some 13 million workers—roughly one in four—couldn't find jobs. It was also a time of severe droughts, and when farmers with failed crops couldn't pay their loans, banks foreclosed on their mortgages—taking away family homes and farms. To many poor people, the banks were deeply unpopular: they represented the rich who ignored the homeless and hungry.

Ohio. He was taken north to Lima, where he would await his trial in the old county jail. Police thought that was the end of Dillinger's crime spree. They would soon learn it had only begun.

There was something the police didn't realize. A few days before his arrest, Dillinger had smuggled guns into the Indiana State Prison, hiding them in spools to be delivered to the shirt-making plant inside, where his friends worked. Using the guns, 10 prisoners escaped. Among them were four men who had plans with Dillinger.

On the night of October 12, the sheriff at the Lima jail sat reading a newspaper, his wife doing crossword puzzles at his side. Three men entered his office. They claimed to be officials from the Indiana State Prison; they'd come to question John Dillinger. When the sheriff asked to see some identification, they shot and fatally wounded him. Taking his keys, the men freed Dillinger, locking the sheriff's wife and his deputy in jail cells.

On the loose and reunited with his prison pals, Dillinger wasted no time. Two nights later, his armed gang raided the first of three police stations and made off with pistols, rifles, machine guns, and ammunition—as well as bulletproof vests. Now they were better armed and protected than most police in small towns across the state.

Newspapers ran hair-raising stories about "Dillinger's gang"— they were a band of desperate outlaws who had vowed never to be captured alive, reporters said; they had bulletproof cars with portals for machine guns in the rear. Much of what was reported was exaggerated or even imaginary (the bullet holes in one of Dillinger's abandoned getaway cars proved that), but the "terrible gang's" almost nonstop string of robberies was very real, and police vowed to end it. As a grim reminder, several police departments placed Dillinger's picture on their firing-range targets.

Dillinger's next heist, in Racine, Wisconsin, did not run smoothly. The teller, his head bowed while counting cash, did not respond when gang member Charles Makley told him to put his hands in the air. Makley didn't bother to repeat himself and shot the teller, who, as he fell, managed to set off the alarm. Ignoring the deafening clang of the bell, Dillinger ordered the bank president to open the vault and proceeded as planned. Drawn by the noise, a curious crowd gathered outside. When the police arrived, Makley shattered the front window with a spray of machine-gun fire, sending people screaming and running for cover.

Slipping away with their loot would be no easy matter now. Surrounding themselves with hostages from the bank, the thieves

WANTED moved outside toward their getaway car, using the customers as human shields from police fire. Officers watched helplessly as the gang sped away with their hostages standing at gunpoint on the car's running boards. Police cars gave chase, swerving to avoid the nails Dillinger's gang threw behind their car to puncture their pursuers' tires. When Dillinger drove over a train crossing, a speeding train blocked the police from continuing the chase. While the frustrated officers watched an endless line of train cars thunder by, the thieves made their escape. The hostages were let go far away in the countryside.

The Chicago police set up a "Dillinger Squad"—40 skilled shooters dedicated to catching the gang. Pictures and profiles of the suspects were circulated widely. Police picked up the fringe members of the gang and pressured them for information, but Dillinger and his closest partners remained elusive. In fact, he and his gang were lying low in Daytona Beach, Florida—renting lavish beach houses under false names and avoiding the danger that awaited them in states such as Indiana and Illinois. Dillinger's restlessness kept him from staying anywhere for long, however, and by mid-January the gang had embarked on a road trip, covering some 4,800 kilometers (3,000 miles) before ending up in Tucson, Arizona.

Partway, Dillinger split from the group and drove north to Illinois. Eyewitnesses identified Dillinger and John "Red" Hamilton (a Canadian robber known by his dark red hair) as the armed men who walked into the First National Bank of East Chicago. Again, an employee managed to set off the alarm, and police and crowds were soon swarming outside. Dillinger's trick of using bank customers as human shields did not protect him so well this time. As he and Hamilton shuffled toward their car outside, one officer was sure he had a clear shot at Dillinger through the hostages. Officer William O'Malley fired—but the bullets did no harm, thanks to Dillinger's bulletproof vest. Dillinger returned fire, fatally wounding O'Malley. Moments later Dillinger and Hamilton sped away.

Dillinger's gang had fatally shot several people during their robberies, but up until now there was no evidence that John Dillinger himself had killed anyone. Now he was wanted for murder, a crime that carried a death sentence.

Dillinger fled south and met up with his gang in Tucson. There, at last, police had an unexpected stroke of luck. The hotel where the gang was staying caught fire. Two gang members paid some firefighters to help them rescue their heavy trunks from the blaze—trunks filled with cash and guns—and bring them to a new address. A firefighter recognized one of the gang members from a "wanted" notice he'd seen at the back of *True Detective Mysteries*, his favorite magazine.

Police staked out the house the two men had moved to. Using a combination of ruses—pretending to be a mail carrier, informing a gang member that he needed to purchase an Arizona vehicle sticker for his car—police arrested four gang members one by one, including Charles Makley. Now only Dillinger remained at large.

Patience paid off. A few hours later Dillinger drove up to the house with his girlfriend and walked up the steps. Two officers were waiting inside the door; a third quickly closed in from outside.

"I must have the wrong house," Dillinger mumbled, turning to leave.

"Oh, it's the right one," the third officer answered, blocking his exit. Dillinger was quickly handcuffed, without any struggle or shots being fired. Officers searched the house and found machine guns, thousands of rounds of ammunition, stolen jewelry, and $25,000 in cash, much of it hidden in coat linings.

Dillinger and his gang were indicted

in a county courtroom packed with reporters and curious onlookers. Some gang members hid their faces behind their hands; others glared defiantly at photographers. It was decided Dillinger would be put on trial in Indiana, where he was wanted for the killing of Officer O'Malley. The other three would be taken to Ohio to stand trial for shooting the sheriff in the Lima jail. Arizona officers accompanied the handcuffed Dillinger by plane to Chicago. On the runway he was met by three dozen armed police officers, and even more state troopers, who took him to the Lake County Jail in Crown Point in a convoy of 13 cars. His trial was set for March 12, 1934. Some grumbled that he should be moved in the meantime to a maximum security prison. But the Crown Point sheriff, Lillian Holley, assured everyone that her jail would hold the criminal.

In jail, Dillinger's captors were surprised by how easy a prisoner he was. He passed the time stretched out on his cot, reading newspaper articles about himself, or joking with the guards. He smiled good-naturedly when they teased him about getting caught. Up close, the so-called desperate outlaw didn't seem so dangerous after all.

On March 3, one of the prison trustees heard Dillinger call to him in a friendly voice. Strolling into the exercise room, he found Dillinger alone and unguarded. The prisoner advanced quickly on him, and he felt the jab of a gun in his ribs. Dillinger ordered him into a cell and locked him in. He then called to the deputy sheriff, and at gunpoint ordered him to summon the guards. After taking their weapons,

STRANGE CELEBRITY

Throughout 1933–34, newspaper headlines focused on John Dillinger—his name sold papers. People were shocked by the audacity of his crimes, but fascinated too. What's more, after Dillinger's Tucson arrest, reporters found him talkative and quotable, even funny. He laughingly admitted he had anonymously sent a police captain a copy of *How to Be a Detective*. While newspapers celebrated the heroic police officers who had brought Dillinger to justice, they also described the bandit's swaggering charm and roguish smile. He was both a criminal and, strangely, a celebrity. Dillinger read all his press, watched newsreels about himself in movie theaters, and enjoyed the publicity immensely.

The Evening Chronicle

SATURDAY, MARCH 3, 1934

DILLINGER ESCAPES

Dillinger locked them in cells as well. With the help of another prisoner, Dillinger next raided the jail's arsenal, then walked the deputy at gunpoint to the garage.

"Which is the fastest car?" he asked the startled mechanic. Dillinger laughed when the man pointed to Sheriff Holley's vehicle.

All four men piled into the Ford. Aiming a machine gun at the deputy, Dillinger forced him to drive them northwest. Dillinger was in high spirits the whole way.

"I did it all with my little toy pistol," he boasted to the deputy and mechanic. He showed them the "gun" he had used to herd the guards into the cells—a crude model carved from wood. Later he released the two hostages near a small town.

It was a shocking escape, humiliating for the police. Sheriff Holley called it "too ridiculous for words" and vowed to lead a search and shoot Dillinger herself. As time passed, the breakout began to look too easy. Had some of those locked-up guards been bribed? Dillinger bragged that he had whittled the gun from a washboard slat, using his razor, but others wondered if it had been smuggled in.

Moments after the deputy and mechanic were released, a widespread manhunt was underway. Yet Dillinger seemed to have disappeared—or rather it seemed he was everywhere at once. No sooner had headlines announced "Dillinger Escapes!" than sightings of the fugitive were called in to the police every few minutes—Dillinger had been seen in different states, in different disguises, each account contradicting the one before.

In his getaway, Dillinger had made one blunder. He had driven Sheriff Holley's car out of Illinois into Indiana. Crossing a state line in a stolen car was a federal offense. Now the Bureau of Investigation (soon to become the FBI) was officially on the Dillinger case. Bureau director J. Edgar Hoover contacted Melvin Purvis, special agent in charge of the Chicago office, and told him to make catching Dillinger the top priority. Purvis was young and completely dedicated to the department. He was also an unmarried man with no family to take care of, who could work around the clock—Hoover's definition of a perfect agent. "Get Dillinger," he told the ambitious Purvis, "and the world will be yours."

Three days after Dillinger's escape, a bank holdup in South Dakota looked like his handiwork. A week

THE BIRTH OF THE FBI

In 1908 a new government agency was created within the U.S. Department of Justice to investigate federal crimes. In 1924 the attorney general appointed J. Edgar Hoover as its director. Hoover had serious ambitions for his investigative agency. He began issuing the first national "Fugitives Wanted by Police" bulletins; he set up a laboratory to pursue the new science of crime fighting—handwriting analysis, fingerprinting, and the examination of firearms. He also founded an academy to train special agents. Hoover could be zealous, and was sometimes criticized for harassing those he considered rebels who challenged authority. The agency became known as the Federal Bureau of Investigation (FBI) in 1935.

later, a bank in Iowa was robbed by the same thieves. Dillinger had evidently gathered a new gang with alarming speed. This one included two old prisonmates, Red Hamilton and Homer Van Meter. Joining them was another notorious criminal, known as Baby Face Nelson. Dillinger led them on a series of heists in different states. His constant movement confused police departments, who at the time did not communicate across states quickly. It was as if Dillinger were making up for his nine years in prison with one long, reckless spree of violence and lawbreaking—a road trip of bank robberies, jailbreaks, and shoot-outs with police.

Purvis issued wanted posters offering a generous reward for information leading to Dillinger's capture. A suspicious landlady in St. Paul, Minnesota, phoned the local FBI office with a tip: she had doubts about her new tenants. Their blinds were always closed and strange people came and went from their apartment at odd hours. It was a vague lead, but keen to leave no stone unturned, two agents and a police officer followed up.

As they knocked on the apartment door, a man came up the stairs, obviously headed for the same apartment. Upon being questioned he claimed to be a soap salesperson, who had left his samples in his car. Suspicious, one of the agents followed him back down. In the stairwell the man whirled around and fired a gun. It was Van Meter. Dillinger, who was indeed inside the apartment, fired a machine gun through the closed door. Caught between two gunmen, it took all the agents' efforts to fend off Van Meter. In the confusion Dillinger slipped downstairs and away, followed by his partner. The agents searched the abandoned apartment and found an arsenal of weapons. They dusted for fingerprints and found matches to those on Dillinger's prison record. They'd been so close!

Wounded, Dillinger retreated to the hideout of one of the city's underworld doctors—medical practitioners who, having lost their license through malpractice, treated criminals for steep fees.

When Hoover learned Dillinger had slipped past his agents,

he was furious: his new FBI's reputation was at stake. "No one has ever shot at any of our agents and got away with it!" he bellowed. "We run them to earth." He urged Purvis to work the agency's list of snitches from the underworld—and if he didn't have enough contacts, to find more! Offer rewards; make threats—*someone* knew where Dillinger was. Purvis and his agents began by going after the fugitive's known connections and less important gang members, who were easier to catch. From there they planned to move inward toward the main prize, Dillinger himself.

Hoover liked to portray his agents as scientific crime-fighters, painstakingly gathering and combing evidence, methodically working contacts for information. In fact, many were young and earnest but completely new to police work. In the hunt for Dillinger, their amateur blunders cost them dearly. When it occurred to agents to check out the home of Dillinger's father and sister in Mooresville, they found that Dillinger had just left. In Chicago they managed to arrest Dillinger's girlfriend, Billie Frechette, but missed Dillinger, who was waiting for her in their car.

On a Sunday afternoon in April 1934, Melvin Purvis got a call. On the line was a man from the small town of Rhinelander, Wisconsin, with an intriguing tip. His sister-in-law and her husband ran a little resort. It was off-season, and when he stopped by he was surprised to see that 10 people had checked in. His sister-in-law secretly passed him a note. It was Dillinger's

> In one of their most embarrassing mistakes, FBI agents arrested a woman they believed to be Dillinger's girlfriend. She turned out to be Betty Karp Marx, the wife of Chico Marx—of the famous comedy group the Marx Brothers.

A MODERN ROBIN HOOD?

When a reporter described Dillinger as a modern-day Robin Hood, Hoover fumed: "The man is a thug!" But in Mooresville, Dillinger's hometown, a movie theater audience cheered when Dillinger appeared on a newsreel before the show—and hissed when Hoover and his FBI agents were shown. One person wrote to their local newspaper: "Dillinger did not rob poor people. He robbed those who became rich by robbing the poor. I am for Johnnie." A prison warden's daughter who'd known Dillinger said he was just a "spoiled boy who wanted attention."

They seemed to forget the fatal shootings at Dillinger's hands (and the fact that unlike Robin Hood, he never gave any of his loot to the poor).

gang, and she didn't dare call anyone. He had driven to the nearest town to contact the FBI.

Purvis's instinct told him this was a real lead. He quickly phoned agents in three different cities and ordered them to charter flights to Rhinelander immediately. Director Hoover ordered that no local police be notified—only his agents could be trusted with such a mission.

The same day, over 20 agents gathered in Rhinelander and set out in cars for the secluded resort known as Little Bohemia Lodge. It was already dark as Purvis and his men drove through the woods. The muddy road was in bad shape, and two cars skidded off into ditches. But there was no time to lose—a last-minute tip had warned them that the gang might leave that night. The agents climbed onto the running boards of the remaining cars and sped on.

Still some distance from the building, they turned off their headlights and slowly crawled to a stop. A long driveway led up to the lodge, which backed onto a lake. Purvis's hopes rose: that would rule out any escape route from the back. If all went well, they could surround and overpower the gang without firing a shot. This was the largest siege the FBI had ever attempted, and the final moments before action were nerve-racking. Silently, the men on the running boards stepped down, and the rest of the agents got out of their cars.

After a few footsteps forward, dogs started barking. So much for surprise! Then Purvis spotted three men leaving the front porch. They got into a car and headed down the driveway, straight for the agents.

"Stop!" Purvis shouted. "We're federal officers!"

The car kept speeding toward them. It's Dillinger, Purvis thought, and he'll try to blast his way through us. The agents opened fire. The car skidded to a stop, its door opened, and a man fell out.

"Identify yourself!" Purvis demanded.

"I'm John," the man groaned.

Purvis clicked on a flashlight and looked at the man on the ground. He was elderly, and clearly not Dillinger. Neither was the wounded man still inside the car. Before Purvis could register the terrible mistake, gunfire erupted from the lodge. Purvis and his agents tried to storm the building from the side, but machine-gun fire from the balcony forced them to dive for cover behind pine trees. Purvis heard another car entering the driveway behind them. It quickly went into reverse, tearing away into the night, its wheels screeching. In the darkness, the confused shoot-out continued. Then three men, including the owner, came out of the lodge with their hands up.

"The gang's barricaded upstairs," they said.

Purvis had ordered a tear-gas gun for the raid, and now was the perfect time to use it. That would force them out! But to his frustration he learned that it was still on its way. It was nearly dawn before the tear-gas gun arrived—and failed to work. One agent bravely volunteered to run into the lodge and throw the canister himself. As smoke filled the building, three coughing women staggered out. The rest of the gang was gone.

It had been Dillinger firing from the balcony. He, Hamilton, and Van Meter had jumped from the second storey into a snowbank behind the resort, met up on the ground with Baby Face Nelson, and climbed down to the lake. Running along the shoreline, they turned into the woods and split up, fleeing in different directions. Nelson sped away in a stolen car. Dillinger knocked on the door of a local carpenter's cabin and, pretending he needed to rush his friend to the hospital, borrowed the man's car and sped off with Hamilton and Van Meter. A local sheriff gave chase, and in an

exchange of gunfire Red Hamilton was fatally wounded. Van Meter and Dillinger fled toward Chicago.

The FBI's first big raid was a complete disaster. Dillinger had got away; two innocent bystanders had been shot. The decision not to involve the police looked foolish now. Police roadblocks around the lodge would likely have stopped the fugitives. Both Purvis and his boss, Hoover, were in danger of losing their jobs.

New crime laws were passed to speed Dillinger's capture, including one that allowed, for the first time, the payment of large bounties. It was known as the "Public Enemy Bill," and "Public Enemy Number One" was the label now slapped on Dillinger across the United States. The attorney general announced a $5,000 reward for information leading to Dillinger's arrest and $10,000 for his capture (roughly $174,000 today).

Hoover recruited tougher agents, including Texas law officers and skilled shooters. Gang members were picked up one by one, but once again Dillinger seemed to have disappeared. He was not only lying low, but had put himself in the hands of another underworld doctor. This time he wanted to change his now infamous face. The doctor also scraped his fingertips and treated them with acid in an attempt to erase his fingerprints. Afterward, Dillinger and Van Meter, one of the few of his gang still at large, planned one last heist. It would be different, a mail-train robbery. Then they would leave the country, escaping to Mexico or South America.

On a hot Saturday in July—a year since Dillinger began his bank-robbing spree—Agent Purvis was on his way to meet with two Chicago police officers. In disgrace ever since Little Bohemia, Purvis felt his hopes revive as he listened to their story. They had been contacted by a woman who called herself Anna Sage. She claimed a friend of hers often went out with Dillinger. It seemed Dillinger's restlessness was getting the better of him. Tired of hiding in rooms with closed blinds, he was going out to restaurants, clubs, and especially the movies, which he loved. The officers took Purvis to see Sage, a Romanian who had moved to the U.S. and was now in danger of being deported. In addition to the reward money, she asked Purvis for help with her immigration problems. In exchange she promised to tell the FBI where and when they could capture Dillinger.

Purvis said he would put in a good word for her, but couldn't promise to keep her from being deported. Sage frowned, but at last agreed that was enough. She said that she, her friend, and Dillinger would probably go to a movie the following night. They would either go to the Biograph theater, in the north of the city, or the Marbro, which was downtown. As soon as she knew which one, she would call. Purvis quickly assembled as many agents as he could and pored over maps of the two theaters, their exits, and the surrounding streets. The dangers were evident: the Biograph in particular had rear exits that led to a maze of back alleys. Worst of all, both air-conditioned theaters would be crowded on a hot Sunday night. How could they take Dillinger in the midst of so many bystanders? A deadly shoot-out must be avoided at all costs. No one wanted another fiasco like Little Bohemia.

Early Sunday evening Sage still did not know which theater Dillinger would choose. Purvis and his men would have to stake out both locations, stretching their ranks dangerously thin. Again they made the risky decision not to involve local police. Hoover feared that Dillinger might have paid informants on the Chicago force, and besides, this was the FBI's chance to redeem its reputation. They alone would get Dillinger.

At 8:30 p.m. Sage called again. It would be the Biograph. "I'll wear an orange skirt and a white hat so you can spot me," she said. The agents stationed at the Marbro dashed to their cars and sped uptown. Outside the Biograph, Purvis waited. It was agonizing. Maybe Sage had lied. He began to fear another failure. A few minutes later, he spotted a man and two women, one in an orange skirt, approaching the ticket booth. Dillinger had changed his appearance—his hair was dyed darker, he now had a mustache, and the plastic surgeon had altered his features somewhat. But to Purvis he was recognizable.

It occurred to Purvis that Dillinger, who was known to wear his gun in a shoulder holster, was wearing no jacket that hot night. Did he not have a gun? Maybe this was the moment to arrest him. But the crowd milling outside was too dense; Purvis couldn't risk it. They would wait until the show finished.

Two hours of nervous suspense followed. Inside, Dillinger was watching

Manhattan Melodrama, a gangster movie. Outside, standing by the ticket booth, Purvis tried to stay calm and not fidget. Pacing across the street, two of his agents watched him, on the lookout for the signal they had arranged. When Purvis lit his cigar, it was time to move in.

At 10:20 the noisy crowd began to leave the theater, streaming on either side of Purvis, who scanned the passing faces, an unlit cigar clenched between his teeth. At last his eyes fastened on them: Dillinger arm in arm with the young woman; Sage walking next to her. Turning left as they exited the theater, they passed so close Purvis could almost have touched them.

Purvis quickly struck a match and lit his cigar. The agents stationed across the street never saw it—the crowd was too thick. But in a doorway south of the theater, two new recruits spotted the glowing signal. Dillinger strolled past them, and they fell into step behind him. A third agent quickly joined them.

Up ahead, an alley ran off the street to the left. Just before they reached it, Dillinger seemed to sense danger. He turned, glanced at the agents, and broke away from the two women. Hurling himself toward the alley, he reached into his right pocket to draw a pistol.

"Halt!" called Purvis, who had broken into a run. Up ahead, the pursuing agents fired, and Dillinger fell to the ground. He died within moments.

His death caused controversy—why had they not taken him alive?—but an investigation found the agents' actions justified. Of the three men who fired on Dillinger, no one ever said which one had killed him.

In the months that followed, Van Meter, Baby Face Nelson, and the rest of Dillinger's accomplices were captured or killed. Three were convicted in the killing of the Lima sheriff. The FBI was vindicated at last and, having learned much from its mistakes hunting Dillinger, began to grow into a formidable crime-fighting force.

ADOLF EICHMANN: TRACKING HITLER'S HENCHMAN

NAME: Adolf Eichmann

BORN: March 19, 1906, in Solingen, Germany

WANTED FOR: War crimes; organized the Nazi deportation and execution of Jews during World War II

LOCATION OF CHASE: Argentina

DURATION: 12-year search, followed by 3-year "Operation Eichmann" (1957–May 11, 1960)

LAW ENFORCEMENT INVOLVED: Israeli secret intelligence agents (Mossad)

Tel Aviv, Israel, 1957

"Eichmann—he's *alive*."

For a moment Isser Harel, head of Mossad, Israel's secret intelligence agency, sat stunned. He was unsure he'd heard correctly.

"Adolf Eichmann?"

"Yes. In Argentina."

Across the café table from Harel, his face deadly earnest, sat Israel's director-general of foreign affairs. He went on to say the information came from a German, a public prosecutor named Dr. Bauer who had a secret source in Argentina. The German had shared his secret with Israel because he feared authorities in his own country would fail to see justice done.

Adolf Eichmann, one of Adolf Hitler's top henchmen, had disappeared without a trace in 1945, at the end of World War II. *Twelve years ago*, thought Harel as he left the café. Some had tried to trace him since, but without success. That night, Harel stayed up reading the huge file on Eichmann from Mossad's archives. He already knew that this man had played a key role in the Nazi's program to destroy the Jewish people. But not until that long night of reading did he understand the terrible energy with which Eichmann had raced toward this goal. With every piece of evidence he read, it became clearer that among the Nazis, Eichmann had been the authority on everything to do with the Jews. "His were the hands," Harel mused, "that pulled the strings controlling manhunt and massacre."

How could it be that no government in the world was looking any more for this arch-criminal? Early efforts to track down Eichmann had fizzled, and with each passing year the trail had grown colder. Some shrugged and said he must be dead; others thought it was a lost cause. Even those nations that had once been determined to bring Nazi criminals to justice had lost interest, turning

ADOLF EICHMANN AND THE FINAL SOLUTION

Adolf Eichmann, a salesperson who lost his job during the Great Depression, joined the Nazi (National Socialist German Workers') Party in 1932, and, soon after, the *Schutzstaffel* (SS), its paramilitary corps. By 1934, with Hitler's Nazis in power, Eichmann had been put in charge of Jewish Affairs. At first he focused on speeding up emigration of German Jews out of the country. Hitler saw the Jewish population as a threat to his vision of a racially pure Germany dominating Europe. He passed laws to discriminate against Jews and drive them out of Germany. Throughout the war, this persecution escalated into a campaign to massacre the Jewish people.

In 1942 Nazi leaders held a secret conference in Wannsee, near Berlin, to discuss what they called "the final solution to the Jewish question": the mass deportation of Jewish people to labor camps, and their eventual execution there. No one present objected to the plan. Eichmann was put in charge of organizing all the details of transportation to the camps.

After Germany's defeat and the end of World War II, the Allies (Great Britain, the United States, the Soviet Union, and France) founded an international military tribunal to bring Nazi military personnel to trial for "war crimes": acts that violate international standards of conduct during a war. These include wanton violence against civilians. But by the time the trials were underway, Eichmann had disappeared.

MOSSAD

Israel's most important intelligence agency, Mossad (short for "Central Institute for Intelligence and Security" in Hebrew), was founded by Isser Harel in 1951. Mossad is responsible for espionage, gathering foreign intelligence, and covert operations outside Israel.

their attention to present-day matters. The war was over, and so were the war crime trials, they seemed to think. The rest of the world might have moved on, but if there was even a chance Eichmann was alive, how could Harel live with himself if he did nothing? By the time dawn began to light his study, Isser Harel had come to a decision: Mossad would hunt down and capture Adolf Eichmann, even if they had to do it alone.

But finding Eichmann wasn't going to be easy. Dr. Bauer was reluctant to reveal the name of his source. Finally, though, he directed them to a Jewish German man living near Buenos Aires. His daughter had briefly dated a young man called Nicolas Eichmann, who wouldn't tell her his address. He once mentioned that his father was a German officer during the war and had "done his duty for the Fatherland." As the boy let slip hints about his past, the girl's father began to suspect Nicolas was the son of the infamous Nazi. In fact, he was sure he had figured out where Nicolas's father was: living in a run-down house in Buenos Aires under the name of Francisco Schmidt. He had come to South America by submarine, the man claimed, and had plastic surgery to change his face. It seemed like a promising lead, but the Israeli agent sent to investigate hit a dead end. Dr. Bauer's source was wrong about Schmidt, and that cast doubt on the rest of his theory.

Yet Harel couldn't stop thinking over the daughter's story about Nicolas. It rang true. Eichmann's wife, Vera, and their sons had disappeared suddenly from Europe in the early 1950s. They could have joined Eichmann, already in South America. The oldest son, Klaus, would be a young man now, and might very well call himself Nicolas. It did seem odd that he would admit to the name "Eichmann" if his father were in hiding, but perhaps he had grown careless. Mossad began investigating Vera's relatives still in Europe, looking for clues to her whereabouts, but anyone who discreetly questioned her family was met with stony silence.

It was not until 1959 that new life was breathed into the search— and again the inspiration was a clue from Dr. Bauer. A new secret source told him that Eichmann had hidden out after the war in a German monastery, and had visited his wife in Austria in 1950. He had sailed for Argentina with a Red Cross passport in the name of Ricardo Klement.

The name Klement sounded familiar, thought Harel. Then he remembered: one of the electrical meters at Schmidt's address had been registered in that name. It seemed like too much of a coincidence. Could Ricardo Klement have been Schmidt's tenant? Even if he was, that was two years ago! Would he still be there? There was another possibility Harel couldn't ignore: Vera might have remarried, and she and at least her eldest son could be living with a man going by the name of Klement. But then why would she take such pains to disappear, and why would her relatives refuse to discuss her?

Harel had been misled by tips before, but this time he decided to trust his instincts, which told him that "Ricardo Klement" was the trail they must follow.

Before setting events in motion, Harel knew he must have authority to proceed. He visited Israel's prime minister, David Ben-Gurion, and told him what he knew. Harel also shared a decision he had made. He did not want to turn over Eichmann to police in Argentina, where many former Nazis had been treated sympathetically. Nor did he want to send him to Germany, where Harel imagined he might easily slip out of police hands with help from old friends.

"I want to bring Eichmann to Israel," Harel declared, "and to have him stand trial here." After all, Israel was now the home of the people Eichmann had victimized.

"If we can do that," the prime minister responded gravely, "it would be a great moral and historical achievement." Both men doubted Argentina would ever agree to surrender Eichmann to Israel. But sending Israeli agents to capture Eichmann in a foreign country without permission would take them into dangerous waters. It would anger Argentina, and the world might condemn Israel for its actions. And yet there seemed to be no alternative—except to let Eichmann go free, which Harel could not do.

Ben-Gurion wanted a legal opinion. The government's legal adviser was shocked by the bold scheme, but after poring over his law books, he looked up and said, "It can be done." He had one condition, though. If Harel's agents captured the wrong man, they must release him immediately and pay him compensation. Harel agreed.

He assigned the best investigator he knew, Zvi Aharoni, to pick up the trail. Aharoni could be relied upon to be purely logical, and, most important, to be secretive—under no circumstances could the true reason for his inquiries leak out. With so many Germans—and former German officers—living in Argentina, there was no way of knowing who was helping the fugitive Nazi. If Eichmann heard or suspected someone was looking for him, he would no doubt vanish once again.

When Aharoni left for Argentina in February 1960, his first task was to find out if Klement was still living in Schmidt's house and, if not, where he had gone. Next, he must somehow prove that Klement was Adolf Eichmann. It wouldn't be easy. There were no fingerprints on file, and their only photos of Eichmann were old ones from the war years, mostly blurred. Aharoni knew he needed helpers, ones who spoke Spanish fluently and who could blend in. He enlisted volunteers through a trusted contact at the Israeli embassy in Buenos Aires.

Pretending to track down heirs for an inheritance, Aharoni first determined that Klement no longer lived at Schmidt's house. In fact, it was vacant and a painter was working inside, preparing it for new tenants. Glancing over his case files, Aharoni noticed that it happened to be Klaus Eichmann's birthday, March 3. He set out at once to buy an expensive present and card, and had a woman from the embassy inscribe it in Spanish, "For my friend Nicki, in friendship, on his birthday."

The next day, Aharoni sent one of his volunteers on an errand. For this one he chose a young man of 18 who was especially harmless looking and always smiling. He was to try to deliver the gift and note to Nicolas Klement at Schmidt's house. Aharoni hoped using the name Klement would be less likely to make Klaus—or his father—suspicious.

"Say a friend who works at a hotel asked you to deliver it," he instructed, "and that it's from a hotel guest. If he's not living there, ask around to find out where he has gone, and come and tell me everything."

Aharoni's young helper also found the house empty, but questioned the workers he encountered, including the painter. When he asked for Nicolas Klement, they asked, "The German? The one with three grown sons and a little one?" The young man shrugged.

The painter said they had moved out nearly three weeks ago, but he did not know the new address. He thought they might have gone to San Fernando. Then his eyes lit up.

"Wait—the son still works nearby. I'll show you."

Together they headed to a car repair shop, where they found a blond youth in overalls. "That's him," said the painter. To the messenger's questions, the young man would answer only that his family had moved, but he took the package.

Aharoni listened closely to the account of events his helper gave when he returned, asking him to repeat everything and taking notes. "While we were talking, his boss called him Tito, or something like that," the young man suddenly recalled.

Aharoni's pen slipped. He knew that Klaus had a younger brother, Dieter. Could it have been him? Was it possible his Spanish-speaking helper had misheard the name?

Aharoni decided to trail "Tito," who rode a scooter to work. Waiting in a car on the road between the workshop and San Fernando, he caught sight of a blond rider on a scooter and followed at a distance—only to be cut off by a passing funeral procession. He waited days for another glimpse. Once again he tailed a blond youth on a scooter, then realized he was following the wrong person. Bad luck seemed to dog him, yet he didn't dare get any closer. He decided to send his young volunteer back for another try.

Pretending the gift's sender was mad at him for failing to deliver it properly, this time he got an address for Nicolas, and the information that their father was working out of town, in Tucumán Province. "Tito" had no idea when he might return to Buenos Aires. "Anyway, you would have saved yourself trouble if you'd got my brother's name right," he added while scribbling the address. "It's Eichmann, not Klement."

Aharoni was now confident that Eichmann's sons were living in Argentina. But was Ricardo Klement their stepfather, or the war criminal he was searching for?

Aharoni drove to the address in San Fernando. It was a boxy, one-story concrete house, surrounded by empty **WANTED** lots. The nearest buildings were a cottage and a stand that sold food. Aharoni felt doubtful. What about all those rumors of Nazi leaders secretly sending riches out of the country when defeat looked unavoidable, and escaping afterwards? Eichmann was known to have enjoyed power and the good life— Aharoni couldn't picture him living in this run-down shack. Nevertheless, he and his helpers drove by, photographing everything. They questioned the owner of the nearby cottage, pretending to be North Americans interested in building a factory on the vacant land. The owner knew her new neighbors were German, but nothing else. Further inquiries revealed that much of the area was unclaimed—it flooded often and people built there without permission. Aharoni and the others returned in the evenings to watch the house, changing their rental car in case anyone might remember it.

The only inhabitants they spotted coming out onto the porch were a sloppily dressed woman of about 50 and a small child. Could *that* be Vera Eichmann and her fourth child, perhaps born after the move to Argentina? There was no sign of any man living there. Aharoni had a theory to test: the Eichmanns' twenty-fifth wedding anniversary was in two days, on March 21. If Klement were Eichmann, he would surely appear in time for such an important celebration.

The next evening, Aharoni and one of his helpers drove slowly by the house and spotted a man taking down the wash from a line in the backyard. He was of medium height and balding, maybe 50 years old. If he's taking down the laundry, Aharoni reasoned, he must live there. The next day he began a stakeout of the house. Hidden under a tarp draped over the back of an old pickup truck, Aharoni lay on a cot and kept watch through a small hole he had cut. He saw the same man again walk into the house. This time he was dressed in a suit, as if for a special occasion. Aharoni's heart was pounding; it all matched the timing of the anniversary.

At the embassy that night Aharoni wrote a report in invisible ink to be sent back to Tel Aviv in the diplomatic pouch. "I have no doubts that I have seen Eichmann," he declared. While he waited for instructions, he wanted a photo of the man to show Harel. A picture taken from his truck would be useless; it was too far away. Someone Spanish-speaking could get close to Klement without arousing his suspicions, perhaps by asking him some harmless questions about real estate. Aharoni enlisted his smiling young man again, and showed him how to work a briefcase camera—its hidden lens operated by a button on the top of the case. He watched from the truck as his helper chatted with Klement, then waited nervously for six days while the film was developed in Buenos Aires—he had no equipment to do it himself. He just hoped his helper's first attempt at using a hidden camera had been lucky.

The results satisfied Aharoni, who flew immediately to Israel, arriving on April 9. There, Israeli police gave the photos to an expert, asking him to compare them to old wartime photos of Eichmann in his German SS uniform. The expert did not know the identity of the man in the pictures. He first drew lines from the limbs in each photo to compare proportions; then he compared the size, angle, and point of attachment of an ear in each image. The ear comparison convinced him. He was nearly certain it was the same man, although he could not say so without any doubt.

That was good enough for Harel, who decided it was time to put Operation Eichmann into high gear. To wait for an identification beyond doubt would be to risk losing their quarry. Later there would be time to find eyewitnesses who could still recognize Eichmann. If necessary, the final identification might have to take place while the operation was underway, even after the capture.

It was urgent to recruit the right task force for the next phase: the capture of "Ricardo Klement." Harel knew the ideal commander would be Rafi Eitan, a man of small size but a natural leader. Eitan was brilliant at orchestrating the details of any operation, and could stay calm in the most nerve-racking conditions.

Together the two men handpicked a team whose members would each bring a special skill.

"Tell each one their participation is strictly voluntary," Harel emphasized to Eitan. "No one will be forced to undertake a mission this dangerous." Once in Argentina, the agents would have to be completely self-sufficient, without help from official authorities. They would be operating alone, hidden from the Argentinian police. Harel believed it was too risky to involve them. He simply had no way of knowing who was secretly friendly with the former Nazi. If the agents were caught, Argentina's police would consider their covert activities illegal. They could spend years in an Argentinian prison. Even if they succeeded, there would be no glory in their accomplishment, as their names would probably remain secret for years to come.

"None of them will hesitate," Eitan predicted, and he was right. Several of the recruits had escaped Nazi persecution in Europe; some had bitter memories of parents, brothers, or sisters killed in Nazi camps. "Your target," Harel reminded the gathered team, "was himself once an expert in police methods and tracking fugitives. What's more, his actions have demonstrated he is without conscience, and therefore extremely dangerous."

Among the recruits was Shalom Dani, an expert forger. He was to provide all the documents for the team, who would be traveling under changing false names and would need perfect-looking I.D. papers. Dani's method was to travel as an artist, his forgery equipment cleverly hidden among canvases and brushes. People marveled at his ability to hand-paint a perfect replica of typed print—even in a moving car. Another was Zvi Malchin, a strong young Polish man whose older sister and her children had been killed by the Nazis when he was still a child. Malchin had vowed to avenge them, and felt a solemn satisfaction when he learned he was the one who

would physically seize Eichmann. A doctor would also be required to make sure Eichmann stayed healthy during his captivity and en route to Israel, while a female agent would give their safe house the look of a normal household. To Zvi Aharoni's relief, he was also approved to continue in the operation. They would need him to identify Klement before they captured him, and he was chosen to be his interrogator afterward.

"Whatever your personal feelings," Harel stressed to them all, "it is crucial that Eichmann not be killed or even harmed." The ultimate goal of the operation was the trial: Eichmann must live to be judged in court. Finally, their movements must remain absolutely invisible to their target until the moment of capture. If Eichmann suspected anything, he was sure to disappear, as he had done so skillfully before.

In late April the team set out. Each member flew to a different city under an assumed name, and entered South America from a different direction, so no one could link them together. Harel decided to join them, so that urgent decisions could be made on the spot without waiting for approval from Tel Aviv. On the way, Eitan worked on two crucial problems: once they had Eichmann, where would they keep him, secretly and securely, until they left Argentina? And how would they get him out of the country unnoticed?

One possibility was leaving by ship, but it would be slow, and stops at foreign ports were chances for their prisoner to escape. A plane was better, but there were no flights from Israel to Argentina—how could they justify a special flight without raising suspicions? A stroke of luck solved the problem. The 150th anniversary of Argentinian independence would be in May. Officials from countries around the world were invited to the celebration—including Israel. A special flight would look perfectly natural. But now the timing of the capture depended on the date of the plane arriving: May 12. It would have to take off again within the following two days—anything longer would look odd and might cause the aircraft to be examined by airport security. That meant Eichmann had to be captured by May 10, leaving enough time to question him and prepare him for the escape.

In Buenos Aires, Eitan scoured the city for the right place to hide Eichmann until they could get him out of the country. Their safe house had to be big enough to fit the prisoner and his guards, and have space for a secret room where Eichmann could be stashed if local police invaded the hideout. The ideal location would be far enough from the prying eyes of neighbors, but close enough to both the point of capture and the airport that both trips could be made quickly. Eitan faced a setback he hadn't expected: every house that met their requirements could only be rented along with its servants—whether a butler, gardener, or guard. No landlord would budge on this condition. At last he settled on the best candidate, a villa that was too small, and gave it the code name *Tira*, or "palace." He rented two backup houses in case something went wrong.

Once again they staked out Klement's house. For days and nights, agents patiently watched from the raised embankment of the railway line that ran near the home. Despite the rain and the clatter of trains, they discovered an important piece of information: Klement was working again in the city. Each day he returned home on the same bus at around 7:40 p.m.—only once had he been late. A plan was hatched to intercept him while he was walking from the bus stop to his door.

Then Harel broke some distressing news. Officials from the celebration ceremony now wanted the Israeli flight to arrive on May 19. The thought of delaying the moment of capture by more than a week was almost unbearable, now that each player was keyed up for action. Plus, a lot could happen in a week: Klement could change his routine or, worse, return to Tucumán. Harel considered the danger if they captured him on time and had to imprison him for a week while waiting for the plane. Besides the security risk, it would be an emotional torment for the captors. But delaying the capture was the greater risk. They would go ahead on schedule.

On May 11 the agents checked out of their separate hotels, changed their physical appearances once again, and met for a last briefing at the safe house. There they reviewed their final instructions. Above all, once Klement was caught he must not be allowed to escape, even if it meant one or most of the team were arrested.

If *Tira* were stormed by police, whoever was closest to Klement must handcuff himself to him and destroy the key, then explain to police who he was. Anyone arrested must say they were Israeli, but that they were acting on their own, not on Israel's orders. The rest must make their own escape from the country by train.

Seven agents set out in two cars, taking different routes to their target. The first, the "capture" car, was to park along Klement's usual route from the bus stop, its hood raised as if it had broken down. The backup car would park a short distance away, its headlights blinding Klement to the first car until the last moment. They arrived late, minutes before the bus, but the men quickly arranged themselves and waited, breathless. The 7:40 bus pulled in, and each man trained his eyes on its doors. The doors opened and a passenger descended. It wasn't Klement. Two more buses passed, and still no Klement. Had he changed his routine? No one spoke. No one wanted to leave, though each passing minute made their presence more obvious.

Nervously, one of the men in the backup car got out to look around. At 8:05 p.m. another bus approached, and he turned back to the car. From the corner of his eye, he recognized Klement descending from the bus. Leaping into the car, he turned on the headlights.

In the driver's seat of the capture car, Aharoni still hadn't seen anything. Then he heard steady footsteps approaching in the dark. He peered ahead but couldn't make out who it was. Seconds later, he recognized Klement, walking slowly, one hand in his pocket. He leaned his head out the window.

"Careful," he whispered to Malchin, who was standing outside, pretending to look under the hood, "he might have a gun."

Now Klement was right in front of their car. Malchin stepped forward.

"Just a moment," he said in Spanish, then rushed at him. Klement staggered back, and both fell to the ground, Klement crying out in an ear-splitting shout. Aharoni gunned his motor to cover the sound. The struggle seemed to last forever. Another agent grabbed Klement's legs, while Eitan pulled him by the arm into the car. Seconds later Aharoni stepped on the gas and sped off. In the back seat, agents bound Klement and slipped opaque goggles over his eyes. He lay on the floor, covered with a blanket, completely silent and motionless. Aharoni said in German: "Keep still, or you will be shot."

Within an hour they were at the safe house. In the room prepared for him, Klement was shackled to an iron bed. Aharoni checked under Klement's arm, looking for the tattoo showing his

blood type, which all SS officers had. He found a scar instead. Armed with his list of identifying traits, Aharoni plunged into his questions.

"What is your name?"

"Ricardo Klement."

"What were you called before?"

"Otto Heninger."

Aharoni didn't expect Klement to admit his identity, so he proceeded indirectly, asking the man in dark goggles his height, shoe size, and then, suddenly, his membership number in the Nazi Party.

"889895." The reply came instantly. It was Eichmann's number. How many people knew that?

"What was your number in the SS?"

"45326." Also correct. Aharoni's amazement grew. His prisoner was making no attempt to conceal the truth.

"Under what name were you born?"

"Adolf Eichmann." The room fell silent. The tension of the long ordeal seemed to melt away, and Aharoni felt a surge of joy. Without speaking, he reached out and shook hands with the agent who stood across the iron bed.

In the days that followed, the team scanned local newspapers for any reference to Klement's disappearance. There was nothing. Perhaps his wife was afraid to alert the police; if that were the case, it could work in their favor. But the silence might also mean that Eichmann's former Nazi contacts were doing their own investigating, and could descend on them without warning. The waiting was tense. Their best hope was that any Nazi allies Eichmann had in Argentina would be too afraid to risk revealing themselves to help him.

In the safe house the agents took turns guarding Eichmann day and night, never taking their eyes off him. Only Aharoni was allowed to speak to him. Their prisoner had become quiet, as if he accepted his fate.

Everyone was shocked to see the "monster" Eichmann up close. He wasn't what they had expected. He was so very ordinary—that was the word they all used to describe him. Malchin, who had tackled Eichmann, now had the job of helping the man blinded by dark goggles to shave and bathe. How could this be the same man who had brought about so many deaths without mercy, who had used his power so ruthlessly? Now he trembled when someone asked him to stand up.

Questioned further by Aharoni, Eichmann explained he'd been arrested by American soldiers after the war, but had given them a false name. In the prisoner-of-war camp his fellow inmates had done their best to help him remove his SS tattoo, and had furnished him with false identity papers in the name of Otto Heninger. After escaping from the camp, he hid in Bavaria, working as a forester, until he heard about organizations that helped former Nazis flee

Europe. He made contact, got a passport in the name of Ricardo Klement, and left immediately for South America. His family joined him two years later. He hadn't known how to get false I.D. papers for them—that was why his sons still used their real surname. Eichmann admitted he'd been suspicious only once of the Israelis' activities. When his neighbors told him someone had been asking about buying land for a factory, he knew it was a pretense. Anyone could see the area would be a terrible place for a factory—there was no electricity or even running water. As for his war crimes, he insisted he had been but a small part in a giant machine. "I had orders," he said. He asked for a trial in Germany, but Aharoni flatly refused.

The passing days wore on the guards, who felt like they were in prison too. Meanwhile, the plan to get Eichmann on the plane took final shape. Their best hope was to disguise him as a member of the Israeli air crew, so he could board unchallenged in the maintenance area, before the aircraft taxied to the runway. Eichmann promised to cooperate, but they didn't dare chance it. The doctor would administer a drug to make him groggy but not unconscious. The "crew member" would be ill, and unable to answer questions. But what if airport authorities insisted he be examined before flying?

The team doctor advised them to imitate a brain concussion. In a routine examination, it was hard to prove that a patient had not had one. Luckily, Harel had one more contact in the city, an Israeli veteran, who could help them. Harel asked the man to check into a hospital and report that he'd hit his head in a car accident. The team doctor would tell him beforehand what symptoms to fake, and how long to wait before showing improvement. If all went well, he would be discharged with a certificate describing his head injury, along with a medical opinion that he could fly home. Then Shalom Dani would alter the certificate to match their false papers for Eichmann.

On May 18, 1960, the special flight left Israel. It was carrying three extra crew members: a double who resembled Eichmann

as closely as possible, and whose place would be taken on the return journey by the prisoner, and two more agents who would act as Eichmann's guards. Neither the captain nor the officials on board had any idea of the flight's secret purpose.

The return flight was scheduled for midnight, May 20. On the morning of departure, the senior crew members were told their help would be needed, but little else.

"We are taking someone to Israel," Eitan said. "Don't ask questions." Because of the celebrations, police roadblocks had been set up, and security at the airport was tight. The Israelis planned to travel in three vehicles. In the first car, crew members were instructed to joke and laugh noisily as they neared the security checkpoint, as if just returning from the anniversary parties. The second car would hold Eichmann, drugged in the back seat, sitting between his guards and pretending to be asleep—apparently worn out by the same festivities. Eitan would drive the third car, watching closely.

The plane must be prepared to take off within moments of getting Eichmann on board. If anyone were to become suspicious, there must be no time for the flight control tower to cause a delay or for security to insist on boarding. To help ward off interference, the time of departure was publicly announced as 2:00 a.m., rather than midnight.

At *Tira*, the agents began destroying all evidence of their stay. Eichmann made no objection to the doctor's injection and did not resist when they dressed him in an airline uniform. He even pointed out that he should be wearing a jacket like the others, so that he wouldn't stand out. Soon the drug took effect, and he no longer answered questions. He could walk, but only with someone on either side holding him by the arm.

At the airfield gate, security smiled at the rowdy crew and their sleeping friends, waving them through. Eichmann's guards emerged from their car, the groggy prisoner held between them. The rest of the crew formed a tight ring around them, and walked toward the plane's steps.

Standing by the plane, the copilot noticed the crew member leaning on two others. They were practically carrying him—was he ill? Then the leaning man was jostled and his face tilted upward. The copilot had never seen him before. So this was their mystery passenger, he realized. His mind raced with possibilities, but he said nothing and followed as the men mounted the steps. Suddenly a roving searchlight lit them all as if they were on stage. The copilot pressed his hand on Eichmann's back, pushing him up the last few steps and through the doorway. Inside, an agent pulled him on board and settled him in his seat. It was 11:00 p.m. One hour to departure—an hour that Aharoni felt would never end.

Ten minutes later a crew member reported the plane was in takeoff position. Only officials from passport control were keeping them waiting. Aharoni felt his heart pound. What did they want? Had they seen them drag a sick man onto the plane and become suspicious? How much did they know? Maybe they had already summoned the police and were only stalling for time.

Eichmann began to rouse, and dark goggles were once again placed over his eyes. He asked questions about the plane, obviously concerned: How many engines did it have? Was it powerful enough to take them to Israel? The doctor examined him and found him to be unharmed by the drug. Beneath them they felt the plane moving down the runway, then turning slightly and stopping. The engines roared, then grew quieter.

Aharoni, like every agent around him, sat tensed, willing his muscles to relax, his mind to be patient. More minutes passed, which felt like hours, and still no movement. What was going on? Outside the window, he could see two men striding toward their plane. The first man broke into a run. He wasn't in a uniform—was he plainclothes security? Had the control tower radioed the pilots to stop?

The roar of the engines increased. Suddenly they were moving again, picking up speed. At five minutes after midnight they were in the air, the lights of Buenos Aires soon fading in the distance.

In Israel, Eichmann was identified by eyewitnesses who had met him before the war. Once announced, his capture unleashed a storm of controversy. Israel's prime minister wrote to Argentina's president, asking him to understand that while laws had been broken, a higher moral goal had been achieved. Argentina was unconvinced and brought a complaint against Israel to the United Nations, declaring that the "illicit and clandestine" capture had violated its sovereignty. UN members passionately debated the case. Did Eichmann's terrible crimes justify Israel's actions? Would approving of the capture set a dangerous precedent, encouraging others to ignore the sovereignty of foreign countries? In the end, the UN Security Council decided Argentina's complaint was just, and for a time Argentina cut off relations with Israel. Around the world, many believed Eichmann should be returned to Germany for trial, or appear before an international court.

Nonetheless, in April 1961 Eichmann was put on trial for war crimes and crimes against humanity—in Israel. During the eight-month trial, witnesses recounted his role in the Nazi program to destroy the Jewish people of Europe, and the generation born after the war received an unforgettable lesson. Eichmann was defended by a team of German lawyers. Enclosed in bulletproof glass, he testified that he had only been following his orders, and was not ultimately responsible. The three judges found him guilty, and sentenced Eichmann to death by hanging, which took place on May 31, 1962—the only execution in Israel's history. His ashes were scattered at sea.

AFTERMATH

Over 50 years later, people are still debating the long-term impact of Eichmann's shocking capture and trial. Clearly, it made a mark on the world in three important ways. The trial drew worldwide attention to the stories of survivors of Nazi persecution. It revived the pursuit of war criminals and fueled the study and prosecution of the crime of genocide (the deliberate destruction of a group). Eichmann's trial also set an important legal precedent by rejecting his defense that he was only following orders and so was not responsible for crimes masterminded by his superiors.

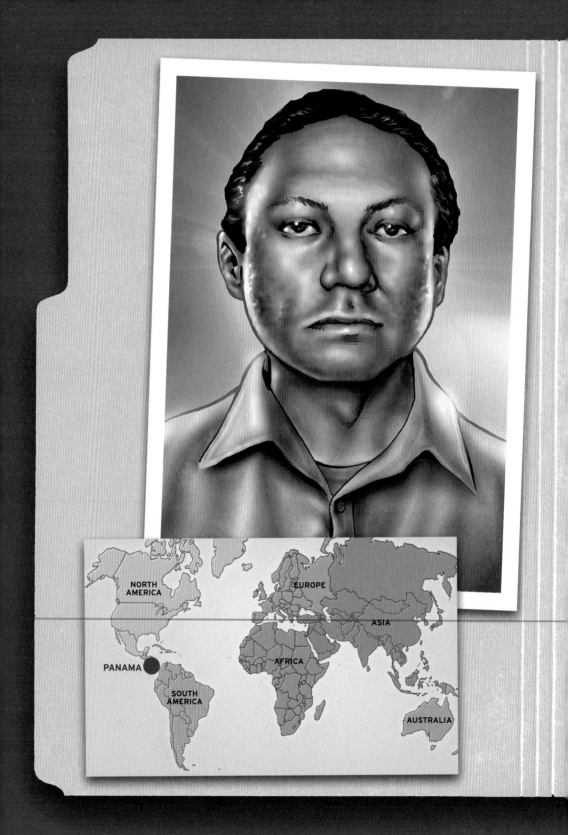

MANUEL NORIEGA: BRINGING DOWN A DICTATOR

NAME: Manuel Antonio Noriega Morena

BORN: February 11, 1934, in Panama City, Panama

WANTED FOR: Drug trafficking, illegal seizure of power, murder of political opponents, rigging elections

LOCATION OF CHASE: Panama

DURATION: 14 days (December 20, 1989– January 3, 1990)

LAW ENFORCEMENT INVOLVED: U.S. military invasion of around 21,000 soldiers, including Special Operations Forces

NORIEGA: BRUTAL RISE TO POWER

In 1981 the leader of Panama's military dictatorship was killed in a plane crash. Colonel Manuel Noriega, the chief of military intelligence, took over the military and ultimately the country. He renamed the National Guard the Panamanian Defense Forces (PDF), and they became his means of wielding power. Within the PDF, two squads were especially feared. Noriega's "Dignity Battalions" were known for intimidating political opponents with violence, and his "Macho de Monte" (Mountain Men) were a disciplined infantry unit whose sole purpose was to protect Noriega. Noriega was suspected of murdering opponents and of drug trafficking, but he ruthlessly suppressed any protests against him.

In the 1989 elections, Guillermo Endara won the presidency by a wide margin, but Noriega ordered his forces to seize the ballot boxes, cancel the election, and attack Endara's supporters. Noriega installed an old classmate as the new president, and continued to rule the country behind a "puppet" government with no real power.

Panama, 1989

Through the night of December 19, more than 20,000 American troops braced themselves for action. Their commanders tracked the passing minutes that brought them closer to H-Hour, the name for the moment chosen to launch their mission—the largest U.S. military operation since the Vietnam War. At 1:00 a.m. on December 20, they would descend on the country of Panama in massive force. A single objective would define the mission's success or failure: remove the dictator Manuel Noriega from power.

Four thousand of the troops were special operations commandos—Delta Force, Green Berets, Navy SEALs, Rangers. At the same moment, each of these teams would hit a separate target. Command knew they had to overcome two potentially deadly disadvantages. First, the timing of H-Hour had been leaked; the enemy knew they were coming. And second, despite an all-out effort by American intelligence, they had no idea where Noriega was.

The decision to invade the Central American country had been a difficult one. The United States and Panama had had close ties ever since Panama's independence and the building of the Panama Canal. Access to the canal was important to the Americans—for both trade and military strategy. It was definitely in their best interests to see the true winners of Panama's election installed in government. Noriega was as dangerous and unpredictable as a loose cannon, and wanted in the U.S. for crimes such as drug trafficking. But they weighed their options carefully. Any raid by a small commando force to capture the strongman was considered unlikely to succeed, and the idea was soon discarded. A better plan might be sanctions against the country—denying trade and withholding canal fees—to pressure Noriega to step down.

At the same time as it imposed sanctions, the American government also let Noriega know that if he left and took refuge in another country, the U.S. would not interfere. But Noriega remained defiant: while the U.S. sanctions hurt the poor in Panama, he and his cohorts relied on the wealth they'd gained through the illegal drug trade. Oddly, he appeared unconcerned about making an enemy of the U.S. Possibly he believed the threats were bluster and that the U.S. government would never resort to armed force to oust him. And he considered himself a man who never backed down. In public, he was always seen strutting in his khaki uniform, his broad, pock-marked face set in a threatening scowl.

There remained one last hope: Noriega's own people might lead a coup against him. Other than his henchmen, who hoped to share his power and wealth, most Panamanians resented Noriega's greed and crimes. In October 1989 it seemed Noriega's enemies at home would indeed solve the

THE PANAMA CANAL

The Panama Canal is a human-constructed waterway that cuts across Panama, joining the Atlantic and Pacific oceans. A ship sailing from the east to west coast of North America saves 15,000 kilometers (9,300 miles) by using it rather than rounding South America. Built by the United States, it remained under that country's control from its opening in 1914 until 1979. A treaty with Panama also gave the Americans control of the 16-kilometer (9-mile) strip of land bordering the canal, and guaranteed them the right to protect and defend it against any armed threat. During Noriega's time in power, the canal was controlled jointly by the United States and Panama, and has since come completely under Panama's authority. At the time of the Noriega manhunt, around 35,000 U.S. citizens lived and worked in Panama.

problem. Major Moises Giroldi led a bloodless coup—his men seized Noriega's headquarters and locked Noriega in a room, hoping to convince him to step down. But they made a huge blunder: Noriega's room contained a telephone. The enraged commander called his loyal troops, who freed him.

In the middle of December, the dictator brought the tense situation to a head. He ordered his puppet government to declare him the "Maximum Leader" and head of state. In case anyone might underestimate Noriega's willingness to use violence, he carried a machete as he took his place at the head of the National Assembly. Panama, his government also declared, was at war with the United States. The next evening, an American officer was killed by Noriega's Panamanian Defense Forces. The American government decided they were now justified in taking action—to defend the canal and Americans living in Panama, and to arrest Noriega for his crimes.

But they faced a frustrating challenge: Noriega was nearly impossible to find. His life revolved around hiding. He never slept in the same house two nights in a row. He rode in one of a fleet of identical limousines to confuse any would-be attackers. The U.S. Southern Command (responsible for defending the canal) was always tracking him, and although they knew much about his movements, it was impossible for them to say with certainty exactly where he would be at a specific time.

If the U.S. military couldn't get Noriega with a surgical strike, they would have to do it with a hammer blow. Their strategy was twofold: harass and weaken the Panamanian Defense Forces, and cut off Noriega's possible escape routes from the country. They

might not be able to pinpoint Noriega's location, but they could make his escape impossible. Once the invasion had begun, Noriega might try to flee by sea or by air, so both routes must be blocked. In case he did manage to take off in a plane, a plan was hatched for fighter planes to intercept his jet in midair, forcing it to land.

H-Hour arrived. Seconds after 1:00 a.m., more than a thousand U.S. Army Rangers descended from the skies in parachutes. They jumped at a low altitude, which meant a shorter descent and less time exposed to enemy fire, but also a rough landing. The paratroopers hit the ground hard, suffering four casualties and many broken legs. Uninjured Rangers quickly secured an important airfield, blocking all incoming roads.

Meanwhile, a stealth bomber flew over the barracks of the Macho de Monte infantry, nestled in the mountainous rainforest. At the same moment as the Rangers' descent, the aircraft  dropped its explosives. The blasts were meant to sow confusion among the sleeping troops on the ground. Another battalion of

parachuting Rangers followed. But Noriega's Mountain Men were wide awake and waiting for them—American troop movements had been reported on TV by the U.S. news. The first wave of paratroopers met heavy gunfire. Yet despite the enemy's advantage, the Rangers overpowered the Mountain Men after a few hours of fighting. Those who didn't surrender escaped into the dense jungle growth surrounding the scene of battle.

A little earlier, Navy SEALs had made their silent way in rubber craft to docks in Panama City's harbor. In scuba gear they swam to Noriega's most likely escape boat and set it with explosives, timed to detonate at 1:00 a.m. Their operation went smoothly. Another SEAL team was dropped close to shore and headed to the city's airport. Their objective: to destroy Noriega's jet with rockets. They were not as lucky. The team was spotted by an airport guard and a shoot-out ensued, killing four of the SEALs and wounding more.

Resistance was strongest at Noriega's Panama City headquarters, the Comandancia, where his troops held out against the siege for 24 hours. By the morning of December 21, Noriega's forces had scattered and fled. In the city streets, some Panamanians cheered the U.S. troops—who remained wary, as the cheers were still followed by occasional sniper shots from buildings. The remnants of the Dignity Battalions were carrying on the fight.

A dozen U.S. military teams had hit their targets with precision and success, but they still did not have their main objective: Noriega. In fact, he and some of his men had made a desperate dash for the airfield in a convoy of SUVs, hoping to reach it before it could be cut off by the Rangers. Spotting the U.S soldiers already blocking the perimeter, Noriega ordered the drivers to pick up speed and force their way through. When the lead car had its tires shot, however, Noriega's driver braked, spun his car around, and fled.

With Noriega in hiding, the real winner of the election, Endara, was now free to take his rightful place as president. But for the U.S., the mission would not be a success until Noriega himself was caught. While Noriega was on the loose, the new government remained in danger. Noriega, so skilled at hiding, could easily emerge for guerilla attacks with his loyal henchmen. He might even go to Cuba or Nicaragua, and wage war on Endara's government from there.

The U.S. offered a $1 million bounty for information leading to Noriega's capture. Tips poured in by the hundreds from the fallen dictator's many enemies, and American officials in Panama and Washington waded through them.

Delta Force took on the hunt. Over the next four days, equipped with sophisticated tracking devices, night-vision goggles, and stun grenades, commandos raided over 40 suspected safe houses. Sometimes they were tantalizingly close—at one house they found coffee cups still warm. It seemed their information was always just a little old. The soldiers kept following tips from local informants or intelligence agents, and found clues that gave them disturbing insight into the dictator's mind. Portraits of Hitler, voodoo altars, weapons, and millions of dollars in cash lay scattered in the empty hideouts.

Among the men hiding with Noriega, some were ready to give up. On Christmas Eve, one of Noriega's trusted captains left the dictator at his hiding spot and set out to contact the U.S. commanders.

He was ready to turn over Noriega, but could find no one who spoke Spanish until it was too late—the nervous fugitive had moved on. The same day, however, the commander of the American troops, Major General Marc Cisneros, got a surprising phone call.

It was Monsignor José Laboa, the Pope's official representative in Panama. Manuel Noriega had contacted him by phone. He had given Laboa a choice: either provide refuge in the Vatican embassy, or watch as he "continued his struggle" by leading a guerilla war.

"You have 10 minutes to decide," Noriega said.

Laboa pictured the deaths that could follow his refusal. He dared not turn him away. Now, in hushed tones, Laboa told the American general that Manuel Noriega had just walked into the Vatican's embassy.

U.S. soldiers had been guarding various embassies in Panama City, in case Noriega decided to take refuge in one of them. The Americans could not seize him while he was under the protection of a foreign government's diplomats. But they had not considered the Vatican's embassy.

Even so, Delta Force had almost stopped Noriega in time. They received a last-minute warning that Noriega was driving to the Vatican embassy, and trailed him in helicopters. Landing outside the compound, they arrived moments too late to stop his entrance. The U.S. government contacted the Vatican and asked officials there to deny asylum to Noriega. Their answer was no: they would urge him to surrender, but not force him.

The days that followed turned into a battle of

> Vatican City in Rome is the seat of the Roman Catholic Church and residence of the Pope, the head of the Church.

> ## SANCTUARY
>
> In a long-standing tradition, churches (and later, embassies) have been respected as a place of refuge for a wanted criminal. This safe place beyond the reach of arrest is known as sanctuary, or asylum.
>
> For hundreds of years, sanctuary served an important purpose: preventing revenge or execution without a trial. By granting a temporary reprieve, it was hoped cool-headed reason would prevail. Today, sanctuary is no longer as widely recognized in law. But in recent years churches have given temporary asylum to migrants resisting deportation, and people fleeing prosecution for their political beliefs continue to seek asylum with foreign governments.

 wills between two unusual opponents: stocky, thuggish Noriega and the gray-haired, bespectacled Laboa. Noriega was not all brawn; he had written a textbook about psychological warfare. As for Monsignor Laboa, he had once served the role of devil's advocate—presenting challenges to candidates for sainthood in the Catholic Church. Both were wily and very confident.

To start, Laboa insisted that Noriega give up his weapons while inside the embassy. Next, he separated Noriega from his henchmen—the dictator had arrived with a small entourage of guards who were also seeking asylum. Laboa's goal was to convince the dictator to surrender, while avoiding any violence. His guest might be easier to persuade if isolated, Laboa reasoned, so he had Noriega's subordinates moved to another building still protected within the compound. His plan was to keep Noriega in a simple, sparse room where, slowly but surely, he would become convinced that his only solution was to give himself up.

The two men had long discussions about Noriega's options. The dictator hoped the Vatican might help him get out of the country, but Laboa shook his head.

"You know, the people of Panama might be outraged if they think you are hiding behind the robes of a priest," Laboa commented. What if a mob stormed the embassy? The Americans would not dare fire on them to save Noriega. Recalling that Noriega loved to read biographies of famous political figures, another idea came to Laboa. He reminded Noriega of how Italy's dictator, Benito Mussolini, was lynched by a mob of his own people. "An undignified end," the monsignor commented. Noriega sulked.

"The Americans might themselves stir up a popular movement to storm the embassy," Noriega shot back later, "and give themselves an excuse to follow inside!" Laboa did not argue with him, but let the idea work on Noriega's mind.

"You can stay here," Laboa repeated again and again. "We will never throw you out."

Meanwhile, outside the embassy compound the U.S. military mounted its own campaign of pressure. Soon after Noriega had entered, the army surrounded and cordoned off the area. When Laboa emerged at the gate to speak to the commanding officer, soldiers realized that the balcony of a nearby hotel was filled with reporters holding microphones. Negotiations or strategy talks must not be overheard, the officers decided. They directed their men to set up loud-speakers and play music to shield discussions from eavesdroppers.

That gave the U.S. Psychological Operations group an idea. They started playing rock music and turned up the volume to ear-shattering levels. Everyone knew Noriega was an opera lover, and they hoped to torment him. The music continued day and night for two days. Finally, it was Laboa who had had enough—the pounding music was driving *everyone* inside crazy—and at his pleading the White House ordered the music to stop. Instead, the men broadcast Spanish reports of Noriega's remaining troops surrendering around the country, in an attempt to demoralize rather than deafen him. Outside the army barricades, Panamanian protesters began to gather, chanting, "Justice for the tyrant!" The barrage of sound continued. Inside, Noriega was plagued by a nonstop background noise that reminded him of his dwindling options.

As days passed, Laboa noticed that Noriega had become very quiet. His shoulders slumped, the general sat on his cot and no longer

PSYCH OPS: A WAR OF MINDS

Alongside physical combat, modern armies often employ psychological warfare: attempts to demoralize enemies, undermine their will to fight, or even persuade them to see the other side's point of view. At the same time, attempts are made to boost the morale of allies and troops. This war of minds includes the use of print, radio, TV, and the Internet to spread propaganda— campaigns to influence public opinion with information, either true or false. Many modern armies have units trained specifically in psychological operations. Noriega believed it was crucial and considered himself a master.

argued. On the afternoon of January 3, 1990, Noriega said quietly to Laboa, "Your solution is best. I am going."

Stepping outside the embassy in his wrinkled uniform, Noriega was greeted by Major General Cisneros.

"I am General Noriega," the dictator said in Spanish, "and I am surrendering to U.S. forces."

"Your surrender is accepted," Cisneros replied.

Delta Force troops ushered a stunned-looking Noriega into a waiting helicopter. Within a couple of hours he was on his way to Miami to face a trial. Monsignor Laboa breathed a sigh of relief. His adversary had underestimated him, thinking himself the craftier of two. "But," Laboa later said, "I consider myself to be much more the psychologist than he. He is a man who, without his pistol, is manageable by anyone."

"Operation Just Cause," as the American government called the invasion, had succeeded, but at a price. Twenty-three American soldiers were killed, and over 300 wounded. Hundreds of Panamanian troops and civilians were killed in the fighting. The Organization of American States and the European Parliament both condemned the invasion. They insisted it violated international law by interfering with an independent country without sufficient cause.

As for Manuel Noriega, he had lost his brutal hold on power, in the end defeated not by force but in a battle of wills. He was convicted of drug trafficking and other crimes, and sentenced to 40 years in prison. He remained imprisoned in the United States until he was sent to France in 2010 to face murder charges. In 2011 France agreed to return the 77-year-old Noriega to Panama to serve prison sentences for murder and corruption. Many in Panama, which has prospered in  recent years, felt satisfied to see the fallen dictator pay for his crimes in his homeland. Among them was a former government minister whose family was forced out of Panama for opposing Noriega. The general's return, he said, "should finally close a chapter in history that we do not ever want to happen again."

ALDRICH AMES: THE MOLE AND THE HUNTER

NAME: Aldrich Hazen Ames

BORN: May 26, 1941, in River Falls, Wisconsin, United States

WANTED FOR: Espionage and treason; sold CIA secrets to the Soviet Union; betrayed CIA and FBI undercover agents, at least 10 of whom were executed by the KGB

LOCATION OF CHASE: McLean, Virginia, and Washington, D.C.

DURATION: seven years, four months (October 1986–February 24, 1994)

LAW ENFORCEMENT INVOLVED: CIA and FBI agents

Virginia, United States, 1985

In the battle of wits between spies, the CIA (Central Intelligence Agency) finally felt they had the upper hand. Their secret weapon was General Dimitri Polyakov—a Russian officer they had recruited to spy for them. He may have been the greatest Cold War spy the United States ever recruited. For two decades, he gave the Americans a window into the KGB, the Soviet Union's secret intelligence service, laying bare much of its inner workings and plans.

Polyakov had volunteered his services while attending the United Nations in New York City. He loved Russia, but not its Communist government.

Besides their star, Polyakov, CIA agents were handling a stable of foreign agents. These "assets" fed them information from inside the enemy spy organization. The CIA was smug about their inside knowledge—it seemed they knew more about the KGB as a whole than any individual KGB officer did!

Then it all began to go wrong. Polyakov was suddenly recalled to Moscow, and the CIA never heard from him again. Soon another Russian agent was recalled by his superiors. His handlers at the CIA advised him to flee to the U.S. rather than return to Russia, and he followed their advice. Then an American CIA agent in Moscow was arrested walking down the street. Throughout the summer and fall of 1985, more and more spies working for the CIA were arrested by the KGB. Some just disappeared. Often months passed before the CIA heard of the arrest— and the execution that followed. Their smugness quickly turned to panic. What had gone wrong? How did the Soviets suddenly know the identities of so many people secretly working for the Americans?

COLD WAR

The Cold War between the United States and the Soviet Union (as it was then known) was a stalemate between the two nuclear powers and their allies. It began at the end of World War II and lasted until 1991, when the Soviet Union broke apart, becoming Russia and several other independent states. Without engaging in active warfare, each side strategized against the other and built an arsenal of nuclear weapons. The threat of a nuclear catastrophe caused worldwide tension.

At CIA headquarters in McLean, Virginia, an investigation was about to begin. At first the agents thought they were dealing with a disastrous leak. Communications, so carefully guarded with coded language and safe meeting places, must have been intercepted by an outsider. But the search for a flaw in the CIA's security would be in vain. A traitor was among them, smiling and talking to them every day.

On April 16, 1985, CIA officer Aldrich Ames walked into the Soviet embassy in Washington, D.C. With his slightly rumpled suit and dark hair in need of combing, Ames looked more like an absentminded professor than a spy. Bearing an envelope tucked under his arm, he approached the stony-faced duty officer at the front desk. Ames assumed the building was bugged by the FBI, so he did not speak—he just handed over the envelope. He pushed his eyeglasses back into place while the officer turned it over. It was addressed to the local chief of the KGB. Inside, however, was a second envelope, addressed to the same man, but by his code name. That was designed to get his attention. No one outside the KGB was supposed to know it. The duty officer took the envelope with a nod, and Ames walked out.

The inner envelope contained the names of two or three Soviet agents who had contacted the CIA to offer information. Attached to this list was a CIA internal telephone directory with Ames's name underlined to show his

RIVAL SPIES: CIA AND KGB

The CIA (Central Intelligence Agency) is a government agency of the United States whose role is to gather *foreign intelligence*—information on foreign governments and countries—to help the president and government members make decisions about national security. The CIA also undertakes covert (secret) missions under the direction of the U.S. president.

The KGB ("Committee for State Security" in Russian) was a foreign intelligence and home security organization founded in 1954 to be the "sword and shield of the Communist Party" in the Soviet Union. It both gathered intelligence on other countries and undertook surveillance of the Soviet people, watching for potential enemies of the government. Much feared within the Soviet Union, the KGB imprisoned and executed millions of Soviets. At its height, it was the biggest security organization of its kind in the world. When the Soviet Union dissolved into several countries in 1991, the KGB was also broken up, dividing into several services.

COUNTER-INTELLIGENCE: WORLD OF MIRRORS

Intelligence is the gathering of vital information about foreign countries, especially enemy or rival ones. *Counterintelligence* describes efforts to block the enemy from stealing secrets: safeguarding information from foreign spies and spreading false information to mislead them. The mind games and charades used to deceive foreign agencies can get so complex that one CIA counterintelligence chief called them "a wilderness of mirrors."

own position: chief of the Soviet counterintelligence branch. Third, there was a note asking for $50,000.

It was almost too good for the Soviets to believe. The man who knew the name of every enemy agent who had secretly infiltrated the KGB, the official in charge of tracking the Soviets' own covert operations against the U.S., was offering to sell the secrets of the CIA.

Ames waited. He tried not to be impatient; he knew no decision could be made without approval from headquarters in Moscow. Finally, in mid-May, he got his phone call. It was Sergei Chuvakhin, an official from the Soviet embassy, inviting him to meet there. Ames knew who Chuvakhin was. In fact, Ames had CIA permission to try to recruit him to the American side. At the embassy, still mindful of possible bugs, the men exchanged written notes. Chuvakhin agreed to pay Ames $50,000 in cash, and explained that he would act as the go-between. Now and then they met for lunch, each bringing a shopping bag to exchange. Ames's bag held classified documents describing CIA operations and the identities of their secret sources. Chuvakhin brought cash and instructions from the KGB. Back at headquarters, Ames wrote up reports of the lunches for his superiors at the CIA, describing them as attempts to recruit Chuvakhin. He made the meetings sound just useful enough to be allowed to continue, but not so exciting that they might draw attention.

Ames had crossed a line, and there was no going back. Even if he stopped now, his actions could not be undone; he was already a traitor. And there was so much money to be made! At the same time, however, he began to feel terribly vulnerable. What if a CIA agent working secretly within the KGB came across his name and exposed him?

On June 13, Ames left CIA headquarters for his lunch with Chuvakhin. It was easy to leave with secrets on paper. Agents were searched on their way in, but not out. Bag checks had caused so many delays they'd been scrapped. This time Ames carried more secret documents than ever. His shopping bag was filled with evidence that would seal the fate of the most important Soviet informants working for the U.S. Ames revealed them all, and asked for nothing in return. Ames himself didn't fully understand his own actions. It was like a leap into the dark, he would later say; it was irrational. His KGB contact informed him that over $2 million had been set aside for him: "Congratulations, you are now a millionaire!" his operational instructions read. Ames asked Chuvakhin to hand over the cash in installments, which would be easier to explain away than a huge windfall.

For a while Ames felt safer. By betraying the CIA's secret helpers in the KGB, he had done what he could to destroy those who might expose him. Money was flowing in and he enjoyed it—he married his girlfriend, Rosario, and bought an expensive house. Then in early August, his feeling of safety was shattered. An urgent cable from Rome arrived at CIA headquarters: a Soviet officer named Vitaly Yurchenko had defected. He wanted refuge in the U.S. in exchange for his knowledge. In charge of espionage operations against the United States and Canada, Yurchenko was the highest-ranking officer who had ever defected during the Cold War.

When his superior at headquarters showed him the telegram, Ames tried to appear to share his excitement. But inside he was terrified. He knew that within the KGB information was not widely shared, but Yurchenko was important enough that he could know about Ames. Still reeling from the news, Ames was horrified to hear that he had been put in charge of debriefing the defector.

On the way to Andrews Air Force Base to meet Yurchenko's plane, Ames tried to hide his fear from his colleagues. What if Yurchenko recognized him? Would he expose him then and there? Or would he wait? For an agonizing month Ames met Yurchenko at a safe house. Surrounded by fellow CIA agents, he faced the defector across a dining table and interviewed him. Yurchenko, his broad frame looming over the table, never said a word about Ames, nor gave any sign that he recognized him.

At headquarters, excitement about Yurchenko was soon replaced with a buzz of alarm. News of foreign agents' arrests and executions was trickling in. Soon, as many as 20 agents had vanished.

Ames's heart raced at each revelation. He had imagined that the agents he betrayed would be arrested slowly, one by one, to avoid suspicion. Instead, the KGB was nabbing them all at once! Ames scrawled a furious note in his next exchange with Chuvakhin. Why didn't they just aim a huge spotlight on his division at CIA headquarters, he demanded, or put the word "MOLE" on the building in a flashing neon sign?

His fears doubled when he was told he would undergo a polygraph test in May. Ames was about to be assigned temporarily to Rome, and was due for a session.

Ames had no idea what to do. This, he thought, was the end. In a panic he passed a note to Chuvakhin, pleading for advice. He knew that the KGB had studied the polygraph and suspected they had ways of outsmarting the machine. When he read Chuvakhin's reply, his heart sank. The Russian advised three things: get a good night's sleep, be cooperative and friendly with the examiner, and, finally, relax and stay calm. Ames crumpled the note in his hand. *Is that all?* he thought.

Later, though, he decided to take the advice seriously. On May 2, when he sat down opposite his examiner and was outfitted with the tube and cuff, Ames smiled and nodded and did his best to appear at ease. At first all went well. To his surprise, the tactics seemed to be working, even when he was asked if he had ever disclosed classified information. Then a question caught him off guard.

"Has a foreign spy agency ever tried to recruit you?"

The truthful answer was "no"; in fact, Ames had approached the enemy. But when he opened his mouth to answer, he stuttered

DIGGING UP A MOLE

A *mole* is an intelligence officer who works for one agency, but secretly feeds information to an enemy agency. Like a tunneling mole, these spies are often "buried deep"—long embedded in the organization and therefore unsuspected—and hard to find. (According to the CIA, a *spy* is any person who gives secret information about his or her country to another country.)

A *leak* describes any instance where secret information has gone beyond the circle of people who are supposed to know it. It could result from an overheard conversation, an intercepted e-mail, computer hacking, documents left uncovered—or the work of a mole.

CATCHING LIARS

The "lie detector test," or polygraph, does not literally detect lies. Subjects are interviewed while wearing a cuff on their arm and a tube wrapped around their chest. These are attached to a polygraph machine that monitors any changes in heart rate, breathing, or blood pressure that occur during an answer. Since a person who is lying will presumably feel stress about getting caught, changes in any of these body functions (which are impossible to control voluntarily) may indicate a lie. However, the polygraph is not foolproof, as the results are open to interpretation. It can produce false alarms, since an honest person may become nervous, and sometimes results are ambiguous. CIA agents are required to undergo a polygraph periodically, in an attempt to catch "security risks": those who are hiding something.

and coughed. The examiner looked up at him sharply. Ames thought quickly. No, he said, but he was very worried that might happen in Rome. He kept his face blank.

To his own amazement, Ames passed the test. The relief he felt was beyond description. He and his wife left for Rome, where Ames continued to sell information to the Soviets through a new contact. But now his nervousness was gone. Around fellow CIA officers he dropped comments about his wife's wealthy Colombian family—in case anyone noticed all the extra

money he was spending. He bought a Jaguar, and as he drove through the Alps to open a Swiss bank account for his new riches, he smiled to himself, feeling like James Bond. As time passed and no one appeared to suspect him, his confidence grew. It seemed he was the smarter one after all.

Back in Virginia, Jeanne Vertefeuille left her small apartment in the early morning to begin her usual walk to work at CIA headquarters. Always a quiet, reliable employee, she had started as a typist almost 30 years ago and worked her way up to a job as a top-notch researcher. There was nothing remarkable about Vertefeuille, except perhaps her incredible memory for details. This small, gray-haired woman was the last person Ames would ever have feared. But he would soon have cause to.

In October 1986 the chief of counterintelligence staff called Vertefeuille into his office. She had been chosen to head up a small task force to investigate the disappearing agents. The first step would be a careful review of all the case files. Vertefeuille smiled. She understood the chief's outdated thinking at once—he assumed a woman would have greater patience than a man for combing through the mind-numbing details of the records—but she agreed that the answer to the mystery must lie in there somewhere.

Vertefeuille was shown to the office that would house the task force: it contained a safe, one desk and chair, and a typewriter. She sighed. Could they have a computer? she asked. Soon her team included four helpers. With great patience, she created a database with all the known details about each of the vanished agents—names, dates, places. Somewhere in the mountain of data, she told herself, a common link was hiding.

The task force followed false leads and chased theories that led to dead ends. No weakness in their protected communications had been found. The team grew frustrated. What if it was all coincidence? But Vertefeuille had a stubborn streak, and she didn't believe in coincidences. As time passed, the arrests seemed to stop. In fact, Ames had been told by his KGB contact in Rome to slow down the flow of secrets: he was giving them more than they could handle at once! Vertefeuille's stalled investigation lost its sense of urgency, and she was often pulled away to deal with other matters. But she had not given up. If the KGB hadn't eavesdropped on their communications, that meant one thing: a traitor on the inside.

In 1989, Ames was transferred back to Virginia headquarters. Thoroughly confident now, he would pop into the task force room and ask if there was anything he could do to help. "What you've got to do," he suggested brightly, "is look for differences between the arrested cases and those that are still successful." Vertefeuille was irritated by his advice, which was so basic it was a little insulting. She got the impression that Ames thought himself much smarter than either her or Sandy Grimes, the other woman on the task force.

In November of the same year, Grimes was taken aside by another agent. Sheepishly, the woman told Grimes that she'd noticed something odd about Rick Ames and his wife. Before they had left for Rome, they never seemed to have any money. Ames used to drive a beat-up old car; now it was a Jaguar. The couple had a new, big house in an exclusive neighborhood, luxuriously furnished. Ames, as chief of Soviet counterintelligence, would have known all the agents who had been arrested. Considered together, these two facts made her nervous.

Dan Payne, also on the task force, took a closer look at Ames's file. A check on his finances revealed some big deposits of cash, but Payne also confirmed that Rosario's family was indeed well off. And the file showed that Ames had passed a lie detector test in 1986. Ames made it onto the team's file of possible suspects, but remained low on the list. When he passed another polygraph test, he was all but ruled out. The search fizzled. It looked like Jeanne's team had failed.

Throughout the next year, Jeanne Vertefeuille could not shake a feeling of guilt over not solving the mystery. In only a year she was supposed to retire, and she didn't want to walk away defeated. She asked her boss if she could undertake one last search. Vertefeuille expected to toil away alone, but was surprised when two FBI agents,

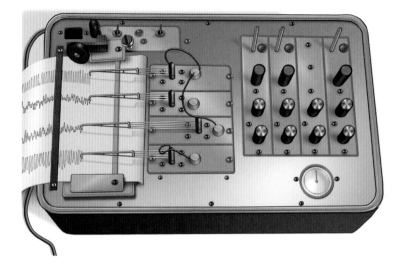

James Holt and James Milburn, asked to join her hunt. The FBI had also lost valuable contacts in the torrent of arrests. Vertefeuille was wary of partnering with the FBI, who were often competitive and mistrustful of the CIA, but soon got used to working with "the two Jims" as she called them. To her delight, Sandy Grimes rejoined the team—she also wanted one last shot at finding Polyakov's betrayer—as did a handful of other helpers.

Vertefeuille started with a clean slate. Her team made a list of every CIA officer who knew about operations against the Soviets in 1985. After ruling out those who had been too far away at the time, she narrowed the list to 160 names. There was no way their small team could investigate them all! She called her people together in her tiny office and suggested an unusual strategy. They would put it to a vote.

"Following your instinct," she asked them, "which five names make you the most uneasy? Which five need a closer look?" She told them to put the one that bothered them the most at the top of the list, and the rest in descending order. After everyone had finished scribbling, Vertefeuille scanned the results. Only Sandy Grimes had placed Aldrich Ames first; Vertefeuille herself had ranked him fourth. She next assigned points to the names listed. Each time a

name appeared first, it got six points, five if it appeared second. A quick tally showed Ames was the winner, with 21 points.

Grimes set to work, creating a long list of Ames's known activities. Dan Payne researched all his bank transactions. Meanwhile, Vertefeuille pursued another angle. Maybe they could find the traitor by finding his contact. She drew up a list of every KGB counterintelligence officer they knew of who held an important position in 1985 and had a good command of English. The list included known aliases and travel. Had any of these agents traveled to the same place at the same time as one of their short-listed suspects? One match came up: a Soviet agent had been in Bogota, Colombia, at the same time as Aldrich Ames. Ames had never hidden this trip; he'd said he was visiting his wife's family. On its own this proved nothing, but it confirmed Ames's place among the top suspects.

By this time Ames had changed his system of contacting the Russians. He no longer exchanged bags at lunch, but communicated through "dead drops." Ames would place a chalk mark on a pre-arranged location such as a mailbox. The mark signaled that a package was waiting in another location, under a bridge or in a drainpipe. The Soviets loaded a separate drop with money and instructions, and signaled at yet another site for Ames to pick it up. They met in person only once a year, usually in Bogota, where Ames would be pretending to visit his in-laws. Ames had no idea that he had moved up among the chief suspects in the mole hunt, and even left a message for his contact assuring him, "All is well with me—I have no indication that anything is wrong or suspected."

Time passed, and Vertefeuille's team still had no proof—about Ames or anyone else. It wasn't until August 1992 that Sandy Grimes made a breakthrough. Working in her cubicle on the painstaking chronology of Ames's activities, she had begun logging his lunches with Chuvakhin back in 1985. Behind her, Dan Payne waded through Ames's bank transactions. Finished with one batch, he piled together the slips of paper and passed them over to Sandy, happy to be rid of them. Grimes entered the bank deposits in her list and suddenly everything became clear. On three different occasions, lunch with Chuvakhin had been followed almost immediately by thousands of dollars being deposited in Ames's account.

Grimes sprang up from her desk, quickly showing the others what she had found.

"It doesn't take a rocket scientist to tell what is going on here," she blurted out, "Rick is a Russian spy!"

The FBI hesitated to narrow the hunt to a single suspect, but by 1993 the two Jims were also convinced by the evidence against Ames. The FBI opened a full investigation of Aldrich Ames, whom they codenamed "Nightmover." Vertefeuille was satisfied. They needed the FBI to make an arrest; the CIA had no power to do it.

Her FBI partners wanted to tread carefully. If anything alerted Ames that he was a suspect, he would flee the country, either to the Soviet Union or South America. With CIA help, they planted a beacon in his car to track his movements. His superiors created a pretext to move his office, allowing the FBI to tap his phone and plant hidden cameras, hoping to catch him packing up secret documents for removal. They even laid some bait, sending him a tempting document and watching him on the camera in his office. To their disappointment he barely looked at it before tossing it aside.

A surveillance team watched his house, and in June they tapped his home telephone. Agents began to search his garbage at night, but had to stop because Ames, a light sleeper, kept waking up and looking out his window. Getting their evidence would take patience. They needed something concrete to justify an arrest—they wanted to catch him in the act. But Ames continued to elude them.

The CIA sent Ames out of town for a conference, and the FBI swooped in on Nightmover's trash once more. This time they struck gold. Ames was intelligent, but he could be sloppy. Once, after leaving a meeting with a Soviet source at a safe house, he had left his briefcase full of secret documents on the subway. This time was even worse. He had begun a note to his Soviet contact, then decided to redo it—carelessly tossing the first draft in the trash. Now it was in the hands of the FBI. Ames had always feared being betrayed by a defector or CIA informant; it seemed he never expected any other kind of danger.

In the note Ames suggested a meeting in Bogota, but stated he would not be able to read any of their signals while he was out of town. He asked them to signal at a drop codenamed NORTH if they could meet. An analyst confirmed it was Ames's handwriting.

There was no longer any doubt that Ames was their mole. They had their first piece of concrete proof! The FBI continued to watch Ames, and, in Bogota, his suspected Russian contact. They had high hopes now of catching him in the very act of meeting and passing documents. But no contact was made. It looked like the meeting had been called off.

Suddenly, the FBI learned they had run out of time to build a case. Ames was planning immediate travel to Moscow. This was their worst fear—Ames could slip away permanently. The arrest had to be made now.

The day before his flight, agents scrambled for an arrest warrant. They considered arresting him on the way to the airport—he might even have an incriminating document in his luggage! But that was cutting it too close. On February 21, 1994, Ames was at home packing when he got a call from a CIA colleague, who asked him to come into headquarters. "We have some hot information," he said mysteriously, as the FBI had instructed him. "You'd better get in here."

Ames pulled out of his driveway moments later. Turning the corner, he found the street blocked by two cars. In his rearview mirror he saw two more cruising up behind him. With a sense of shock, he knew it was over. Ames did not resist. Within a minute, he was handcuffed and under arrest for espionage.

Aldrich Ames pleaded guilty and was sentenced to life in prison, without chance of parole—a sentence he is still serving. His wife was sentenced to five years; phone taps revealed that she knew about and encouraged his spying.

After his sentencing, Ames was debriefed at the office of the FBI. Jeanne Vertefeuille was there to represent the CIA. It was a weird sensation to sit down with the mole she had hunted for over seven years.

"Hi, Rick," she said when he entered the room. As the questioning wore on, for an instant she forgot his crimes. She had worked alongside Rick Ames for so many years, and though she had always found him a little lazy and arrogant, she'd enjoyed their friendly debates. Now she found herself arguing with him in the familiar way they used to. Then she caught herself.

Ames seemed determined to act professional, now that the tables were turned. As he reminded his interrogators, he

> Aldrich Ames is one of the highest-paid spies of all time: he received over $2.7 million from the Soviets, who had an additional $2 million set aside for him. Ames was arrested before he could collect that.

used to debrief agents himself. He revealed the whole scope of his treason, listing those he had betrayed. Vertefeuille felt that for the most part he was telling the truth. When he claimed he was unable to identify his Soviet contacts, however, she sensed that he had switched loyalties. Did he hope they might still help him?

The FBI questioned him next about the flurry of arrests the KGB had made. Ames told them how he had panicked. The KGB, he said, had asked him if there was anyone they could help frame for the treason, to move suspicion away from Ames. Could he suggest a scapegoat?

Ames paused and glanced at Jeanne before adding in an offhand manner, "I told them Jeanne Vertefeuille."

For a moment she was stunned. He had almost made her one of his victims, and now admitted it casually and without apology. Her next reaction was a desire to jump across the table and throttle him. But the urge passed, and she found herself laughing. The FBI agents looked at her oddly, but she didn't care. It *was* funny, she thought, because Ames was sitting there in shackles, not her.

A TRAITOR'S MOTIVES

Like all the agents on the case, Vertefeuille was baffled by one question: Why? Ames had worked for the CIA his whole adult life, just like his father before him. Why had he become a traitor? In 1985 he and his luxury-loving girlfriend were living beyond their means and Ames was deep in debt. Selling secrets was an easy way out. Vertefeuille blamed Rosario, believing Ames would do anything to please her. But Ames hinted that was not the whole explanation.

Although he said his reasons were "personal and banal" and amounted to "greed and folly," he himself seemed confused about his actions. He had spent long hours in conversation with the Soviet contacts he was supposed to recruit. Over time he grew disillusioned with the CIA and its activities. Somewhere along the line he told himself it would be okay to switch loyalties—after all, it was a game everyone had agreed to play. While he realized the people he betrayed might pay for his actions with their lives, he said he simply got used to the idea. "I gave up names of those who had previously given up others," he said. "It's a nasty kind of circle, with terrible human costs." His arrogant explanation seemed like a refusal to face up to what he had done.

To Vertefeuille, Ames resembled the CIA's psychological profile of a traitor, in that he was dangerously self-centered—his own gratification mattered more than everything, and everyone, else.

VLADIMIR LEVIN: CATCHING A CYBER THIEF

NAME: Vladimir Leonidovich Levin

BORN: March 11, 1971, in Russia

WANTED FOR: Computer fraud and theft; robbed Citibank of $10 million by illegally accessing its wire-transfer network

LOCATION OF CHASE: United States, Russia, England

DURATION: 7 months (August 1994–March 1995)

LAW ENFORCEMENT INVOLVED: FBI, Russian police, Scotland Yard, Interpol

Argentina, 1994

On a hot summer morning in Buenos Aires, Carlos Arario had barely settled down to work in his office when he saw something was terribly wrong. The head trader of Invest Capital stared for a moment in disbelief at his computer screen. Then he quickly dialed his boss. "Better get down here," he said grimly. "We've been raided."

Overnight, $200,000 had been transferred out of the company's Citibank account. No one had authorized it. All Arario could discover was that money had been sent in four transfers to four destinations, all unknown. The company director immediately called Citibank's executives in New York City.

Citibank officials tried to calm the irate director, but soon found their own fears mounting. More panicked calls came in from customers whose money had been transferred out of their accounts without their knowledge or permission. And not just in Argentina. It was happening in Indonesia and South Africa as well. Citibank

was the fifth-largest bank in the world, with branches around the globe.

This was clearly no isolated accident. An emergency meeting was called in the bank's Wall Street headquarters to shut down the rogue transfers and control the damage. Experts were summoned to stem the electronic flow of funds. Soon the conference room looked more like a war room. But it was useless. The bank had lost control of its own accounts. The experts and executives watched as money continued to be siphoned out of Citibank accounts around the world.

How was it even possible? Citibank prided itself on offering its big corporate customers fast fund transfers from their accounts to any bank in the world, using its computer network. The customer could request a transfer at any computer linked through the telephone system to Citibank's main computer in New Jersey. Two separate people, usually employees of the customer, had to authenticate the request with their user I.D. and password. After that, Citibank's New York wire-transfer department processed it automatically. Now the system was betraying its creators: the trickle of money leaving turned into a torrent. Money was being sent everywhere—to California, the Netherlands, Finland, Greece, Israel.

Citibank contacted the FBI, and agents

CYBERCRIME: THE RISE OF THE HACKER

Cybercrime is the use of a computer for criminal activity— it might be fraud, stealing another person's identity or ideas, or violating privacy.

Once the Internet began linking computers worldwide in the early 1990s, a new kind of criminal was created: the hacker. Hacking includes any attempt to access someone else's computer through the Internet without permission. Hackers have been motivated by the lure of money, secret information, or sometimes just fame for their exploits among fellow hackers.

Many computer experts insist not all hacking is bad—it depends on the motive. "Black hat" hackers devise ways to intrude on computers to spy, steal, commit fraud, or cause damage. Their hacks are crimes. "White hat" hackers penetrate computer systems to discover flaws in security, and report the vulnerable zone to the owner. Some companies hire white hat hackers as "security researchers" in the belief that it takes a hacker to outwit a hacker.

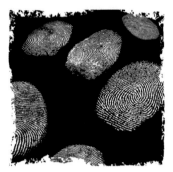 were assigned to solve what looked like the biggest cyber theft they had ever seen. They tried to track the fraudulent transfers as they continued, hoping to catch the thief. But they could not trace the destination of the stolen money. Before they had found a single serious lead, nearly 20 accounts had been raided and more than $10 million had simply disappeared.

Weeks passed before there was a break in the case. At last FBI agents and the bank's experts managed to track one of the elusive transfers: from the account of a business in Indonesia to a Bank of America account in San Francisco. Federal agents decided the right time to catch the thief would be the moment anyone tried to get at the stolen money. They learned the San Francisco account had been opened by Evgeni and Ekaterina Korolkov, a Russian couple who had recently moved to the U.S.

When Ekaterina tried to withdraw cash from the account, federal agents were waiting to arrest her. They felt sure neither she nor her husband were the masterminds of the theft, however. Ekaterina was probably a "mule," an accomplice whose job was to pick up and move the stolen cash to another location. The scope of this crime was worldwide—someone else was surely behind it. During questioning, FBI agents told Korolkov they would treat her case leniently if she helped them find the thief at the center of the web.

Ekaterina finally agreed, and convinced her husband to cooperate as well. Before they had moved to the U.S., Evgeni said, he had worked in St. Petersburg at a small software and trading firm called AO Saturn. The man they wanted was there. His name was Vladimir Levin.

According to Korolkov, Levin had used his office computer to

access Citibank's network. He stole lists of customer I.D.s and passwords. Over several weeks, he logged on 18 times, making around 40 wire transfers from Citibank accounts to ones opened by accomplices in the U.S., Finland, the Netherlands, Germany, and Israel—where the accomplices were waiting to withdraw the money.

FBI agents flew to St. Petersburg and met with Russian police. Since the end of the Cold War, the FBI had been striving to make friendly contact with Russian law enforcement. Now those efforts would pay off. Russian police officers entered and videotaped AO Saturn's office—a small, shabby room crammed with computers. Russian telephone-company workers helped Citibank trace the transfers to AO Saturn, confirming Korolkov's story.

But Levin himself was nowhere to be found. While in Russia, federal agents gathered information on this alleged mastermind. He was a young computer programmer in his twenties, who until recently had been a student at St. Petersburg State Technological Institute. AO Saturn looked like a small start-up company run by Levin and a group of mathematicians and scientists.

With plundered cash moving around the globe, this was an international case, and the FBI could not pursue it on their own. Through Interpol, they asked police in countries around the world to be on the lookout for the mules.

It worked. Police in Rotterdam picked up Vladimir Voronin as he tried to collect $1 million from a Dutch bank. He was sent to the U.S., where, like the Korolkovs, he pleaded guilty and agreed to

help the investigation. "It was not because I liked to do it; I had to do it," he said. It was a mysterious statement. What did he mean? What, or who, forced him?

Catching Levin was turning out to be trickier, however. The United States and Russia had no extradition treaty—an agreement between countries to surrender to each other suspected criminals wanted for a crime. There were limits to Russian cooperation in the case. Levin had committed no crime in Russia, and Russian authorities would not hand him over. As long as Levin stayed in Russia, it looked like he would never be caught.

Levin remained out of the law's reach until 1995. For some reason—perhaps he was lured, or perhaps he made a blunder—

THE MOST NOTORIOUS HACKER?

Despite his record-breaking cyber theft, Vladimir Levin served less prison time than another cybercriminal, who was once the world's most infamous hacker.

Kevin Mitnick, an American, began his online criminal escapades at the age of 17. Still on probation for his first crime, he was caught breaking into university computers, and later hacked into military defense networks. In 1989 he was sentenced to a year in prison for stealing software valued at $1 million, plus three years probation—during which he was not allowed to touch a computer. When the FBI attempted to arrest Mitnick for violating his probation terms, he fled and went into hiding. For the next two and a half years, he was one of the FBI's "Most Wanted" criminals—the first hacker to make it onto their list. Mitnick hid behind a series of fake identities and continued committing his online crimes, stealing 20,000 credit card numbers and valuable secrets from companies such as Apple. With the help of computer expert Tsutomu Shimomura—whose computer Mitnick hacked—the FBI finally caught Mitnick in 1995.

"I never made any money directly from hacking," Mitnick claimed. "I wasn't malicious." After serving his five-year sentence, Mitnick changed his ways and became a consultant—teaching people how to keep their computer networks safe from hackers like himself.

Levin traveled by plane through England. Scotland Yard was working on the case with the FBI through Interpol, and its officers arrested Levin while he was waiting to change planes in London's Stansted Airport.

For over two years, Levin fought his extradition to the United States, pleading that he be returned to Russia instead. His appeal was denied by England's House of Lords in June 1997. In the U.S., Levin pleaded guilty to conspiracy to commit fraud. He was sentenced to three years in prison, and ordered to pay Citibank $240,000.

The Citibank cyberheist heralded a new kind of crime. Instead of sticking up a bank at gunpoint, Levin sat in a room in Russia and robbed an American bank of over $10 million, using nothing more than his personal computer. In the end, Citibank claimed it had retrieved all but $400,000 of the stolen money. It also tightened its security measures, and introduced the dynamic encryption card, which must be physically present when the customer makes a transfer, as it generates a new password each time.

As time passed, some doubted

that Vladimir Levin was the sole mastermind behind the international cyberheist. He seems to have been an average-level programmer and would-be entrepreneur. But was he up to inventing and carrying out a worldwide scheme like this, with accounts and mules waiting in several countries? Various theories have surfaced since. Some claim the secret to breaking into Citibank's system was sold by a Russian hacker ring that had infiltrated the bank's network and was toying with it. They had no intention of robbing the bank, but enjoyed exploring the operating system unnoticed by bank staff. An anonymous hacker who claimed to be part of this group said he sold the secret to Levin for $100. But was the

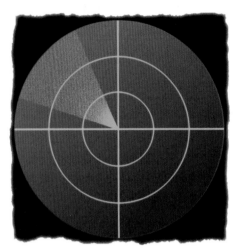

buyer really Levin? Some are sure the buyers were members of the Russian mafia, organized criminals known to be involved with cybercrime. Levin may have been only a pawn in a much bigger criminal game.

If so, the Citibank heist was not just the first and one of the biggest cyber bank robberies. It heralded another sinister trend—criminal hacker rings that, far from being the handiwork of one misfit individual and a laptop, are well-run criminal organizations.

A MYSTERIOUS CRIME

Many questions remain unanswered about the Citibank heist. After Levin's extradition to the U.S., newspapers called him the mastermind behind the first Internet bank raid. Some computer experts disagree. They say Levin really used the telephone system, not the Internet. He intercepted customers' phone calls to the bank and learned their access codes as they punched them in on their telephone keypad. Others insist that Levin must have had inside help, but Citibank has always denied this, saying the accounts Levin raided were unprotected by encryption (a security flaw they have since fixed). No Citibank employee was ever charged.

Exactly how Levin obtained the account names and access codes has never been fully explained. Banks are reluctant to disclose such information, as they would rather not reveal how they were robbed. They also want to protect their image as safe and secure places for people's money. For that reason, it is difficult to know just how much of a problem wire-transfer frauds continue to be.

THE FUTURE OF CYBERCRIME-FIGHTING

The FBI admits that fighting cybercrime still poses a huge challenge. The global scope of the attacks puts law enforcement at a disadvantage. Even though banks have made their computer networks tougher to crack since Levin's heist, other hacker rings have penetrated bank systems. They have increased the amount of money available to an account, or stolen customer information to make phony automatic teller machine cards. The trouble is, the thieves could be anywhere in the world, and after their heist they disappear into thin air, as one agent put it.

The FBI's goal now is to increase cooperation among police forces in different countries, and to change cybercrime laws worldwide to be similar everywhere. That way a cyber thief in Europe who robs a South American bank can't hide from prosecution because of a difference in laws. Prison sentences for convicted cybercriminals are also getting tougher. In the past a convicted hacker might be released on probation, or be sent to prison for several months. Now prison sentences of several years are more common, depending on the damage done by the crime.

CHRISTOPHER COKE: GOING TO WAR AGAINST THE DON

NAME: Christopher Michael Coke, known as "Dudus"

BORN: March 13, 1969, in Kingston, Jamaica

WANTED FOR: Drug and weapons trafficking; murder

LOCATION OF CHASE: Jamaica

DURATION: 31 days (May 24–June 22, 2010)

LAW ENFORCEMENT INVOLVED: Police and army (Jamaica Defence Force)

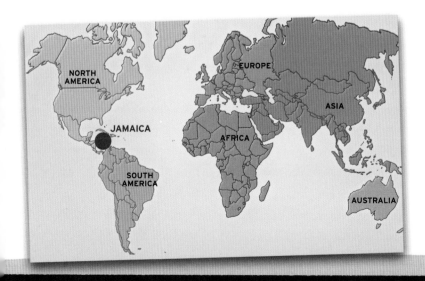

Kingston, Jamaica, 2010

The main streets are blocked with barricades and barbed wire. Sentries toting guns patrol the outer limits of the district. As a Jamaican morning in May grows hotter, an eerie silence hangs over the scene. No shoppers or workers are visible anywhere. The sentries listen, ever alert, for the rumble of army trucks and tanks they know are coming. They watch overhead for helicopters. It looks like a battle is about to begin, but Jamaica is not at war. The armed forces about to descend on West Kingston are not an invading army. They are Jamaican, and they are after one man.

Christopher Coke, considered by many to be the most dangerous and powerful man in Jamaica, was wanted by the United States for drug and weapons trafficking. But arresting Coke was not so simple. The drug lord controlled a neighborhood called Tivoli Gardens in West Kingston, Jamaica, and had turned it into his personal fortress, guarded by his gunmen. Inside the concrete apartment complexes, their walls painted in bright pinks and blues, were snipers and armed thugs—but also innocent families who called Tivoli Gardens home. What's more, many of these people had mixed feelings about Coke, regarding him with a combination of fear and loyalty.

Who was this man an army had been called upon to subdue? The leader of the "Shower Posse"—a violent gang so called because they showered their enemies with bullets—Christopher Coke was known as the "Don" of Tivoli Gardens. Coke was feared, but also depended upon, by many of the poor who lived there. In this community near Kingston's waterfront, "Dudus," as Coke was nicknamed, acted like Tivoli's president. Coke ran the neighborhood like an enclosed state inside Jamaica—places like Tivoli were known as "garrison towns." There, Coke was the law. It was said

police even asked his permission before entering. People feared him, but they also went to him for clothes or food they couldn't afford, for help finding jobs, for loans. If someone in Tivoli Gardens was robbed, instead of going to the police, they saw Coke's people, and often got their stolen property back. People felt safe on the streets and didn't fear break-ins, as Coke did not tolerate thieves in his domain. Like his father before him, Dudus bought loyalty with generous help, and in return expected obedience and silence. And like his father, he counted on the mixture of fear and gratitude he inspired in people.

Dudus's father, Lester Coke—known as Jim Brown—was the Shower Posse's first leader. In his teens, a childhood friend recalled, Lester had avoided trouble. But that changed when he had a harrowing encounter with the growing violence of West Kingston. Gangs tied to rival political parties began fighting it out in the

streets of his neighborhood. Caught in a spray of gunfire, Lester was badly injured, but survived. "When he re-emerged," his old friend said, "he came back as a bad, bad man."

Soon Lester embraced the same violent ways that had nearly killed him. If crime and violence had taken over his community, then he would be one of its rulers, not a victim. He and his Shower Posse began a decades-long reign over Tivoli Gardens, growing rich on the illegal drug trade. During the 1980s, his gang was blamed for at least 1,000 murders. In 1992, Lester Coke was in a Jamaican prison waiting to be extradited to the U.S. on drug charges when his oldest son—the apparent heir to Lester's crime empire—was killed in an ambush. On the day of his son's funeral, Lester Coke died in a mysterious fire in his cell. Christopher, barely in his twenties, stepped in to take his father's place.

He was not the obvious heir. Lester had another son who expected to be the next leader, and he was angry to be passed over by Lester's men in favor of the younger, adopted Christopher. In time the hard feelings subsided, and the brothers arrived at a truce. The younger Coke was a compact, stocky youth with a serious face. Unlike many gangsters, he wasn't flashy or loud. He avoided attracting attention but, surrounded by his posse of some 200 "soldiers," he kept Tivoli Gardens in an iron grip every bit as strong as his father's.

At the same time, Christopher Coke played the role of guardian to the poor of Tivoli Gardens. Each September he paid for children's schoolbags and books. He hosted charity events, sponsored sports teams, and even founded a school to teach youths computer technology. He was a strangely two-sided figure—giving generous help with one hand, threatening violence with the other.

Now Coke's reign was about to be challenged. In August 2009, the United States demanded that Jamaica extradite Dudus to

America. He was wanted by authorities there for smuggling and selling illegal drugs and guns in the U.S. Jamaica's government stalled and made excuses. Even Jamaica's prime minister seemed afraid to interfere with the powerful Coke.

By May 2010, pressure to do something about Coke—and rumors that the Jamaican government had ties to the Don—became too great to ignore. Prime Minister Bruce Golding finally authorized Coke's arrest. The news sent the Shower Posse into action, and Tivoli Gardens braced itself for violent consequences. Stores closed early, pulling down their steel shutters, and people fled from the streets.

Coke ordered his men to turn Tivoli Gardens into a fortress expecting a siege. Barricades of concrete rubble and twisted wire were built to block anyone trying to breach the neighborhood. Shooters took their places behind sandbags.

Yet Christopher Coke was too slippery to stake everything on the outcome of one battle. At the same time as he was preparing for war, he was also negotiating his possible surrender to the police, using a respected bishop as his go-between. Bishop Herro Blair had the government's blessing to enter Tivoli Gardens and do his best to negotiate the surrender. A contact from Coke took Blair inside the fortified stronghold.

"I spent two hours with him," Bishop Blair said when he emerged, shaken by the experience. "I came out, thank God, safely; I can't tell you what I saw, but just imagine what I saw."

He begged the police already preparing to enter, "Please, if you go in, remember there are innocent lives

EXTRADITION: NOWHERE TO HIDE

Extradition takes place when one country surrenders a suspect to another country so that person may stand trial for crimes committed there. It occurs most often when the two countries have a treaty, agreeing to hand over suspects to each other. In the past, some criminals have fled to a nation without an extradition treaty with the country of their crime, hoping to find a safe haven.

Normally the U.S.–Jamaica treaty would have ensured Coke's extradition. However, Jamaican authorities at first refused the extradition request, claiming that the evidence against Christopher Coke (mostly wiretapped phone calls) had been illegally obtained.

Similar to the custom of sanctuary, a church bishop has traditionally been allowed to intercede on behalf of a criminal, pleading for merciful treatment if he or she surrenders to police.

that must be saved." Blair kept in contact with Coke for several tense days. Meanwhile, the women of Tivoli Gardens marched in protest, bearing signs with slogans such as, "Don't Take Dudus from Us!"

Hopes of a peaceful surrender were dashed within the week, when Coke's men shot at police and set fire to a police station. Both sides knew there would be no more negotiations.

Alarmed, the prime minister declared a state of emergency. Police were granted sweeping powers to arrest and hold suspects in custody. It was clear a grim decision had been made. The police and the army, the Jamaica Defence Force, were going to force their way into Tivoli Gardens and seize Christopher Coke. Jamaica was going to war on the seemingly invincible Don.

On May 23, radios and TV stations broadcast an appeal to the people of Tivoli Gardens: any law-abiding citizens who wished to leave must do so now. Police drove buses as close as they dared to the edge of the neighborhood to take people away from the violence to come. Yet only a few boarded. The buses waited, their engines idling, and then pulled away at last with many empty seats. Clearly most residents were afraid or unwilling to use them—afraid of looking disloyal to the community, and the shame that would bring; or worse, of looking to Coke's men like a police informer.

The next morning Tivoli Gardens held its breath. Then, at 11:00 a.m., it began. Army trucks filled with soldiers and police were bearing down on the perimeter. Almost immediately, they were fired upon by snipers. Soldiers poured out of the trucks, and in the shoot-out that followed, bystanders still outdoors were caught

in the crossfire. The rest of the people cowered in their homes, listening to the gunfire. Besides the nonstop gunshots, they heard explosions that shook their walls, and the sound of heavy vehicles as bulldozers forced their way over barricades.

Police and soldiers followed in their wake, pressing further into the neighborhood. They began searching door to door, scouring the apartments for Coke.

The siege wore on into the afternoon heat. As the sun beat down on the colorful walls, soldiers ransacked apartments for weapons and suspects, checking every man's hands for telltale signs of having fired a weapon.

To the police, everyone they met was a potential member of Coke's gang. To frightened people hiding in their homes, however, it seemed the raiding police were not doing enough to distinguish harmless citizens from posse members. Suspects were rounded up and taken to the community center. When the day ended, more

than 70 people had been killed, including at least three police officers. And still Coke was nowhere to be found.

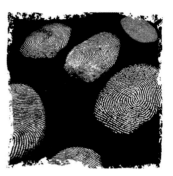

In fact, he was long gone. When Coke and his closest posse members realized there was no chance of holding out against the barrage, they put another plan into action. One by one, they slipped down into the rainwater drains in gullies that snaked through Tivoli Gardens like a maze. While the gunshots rang out overhead, and police searched room after room, Coke and his henchmen were threading their way out from under the siege, surfacing far from the turmoil, and disappearing from sight.

An outcry followed the siege of Tivoli Gardens. So many casualties, so many people taken from their homes as suspects—and yet the Defence Force had confiscated only a handful of guns. Could the Jamaican authorities justify so much force to arrest one man? A man they had failed to capture?

Rumors spread about where Coke had gone, and police chased false leads. Some claimed Coke was hiding on the other side of the island, and police fanned out to search. Others insisted Coke had already left Jamaica by boat.

A month later, following an anonymous tip, Jamaican police stopped Coke's car at a roadblock outside Kingston. They arrested the fugitive without a struggle. It seemed he had been moving continually across Jamaica, changing disguises. When they caught him, police said, he was wearing a wig and baseball cap. Another wig and women's eyeglasses were in the car. With him was a local religious leader, who said he was on his way with Coke to the American embassy to help him surrender.

In June 2012, Coke pleaded guilty to drug trafficking and other charges in a U.S. court and was sentenced to 23 years in prison. "I'm pleading guilty because I am," he said. The guilty plea saved him from a life sentence, and left the possibility that he might live to

return to Jamaica. More than anything, however, he feared dying in a Jamaican jail, like his father—whose death in the prison fire had always haunted him. Before sentencing, Coke asked the judge for mercy, handing him a seven-page letter describing the ways he had helped the poor in his community.

"I concede that he did good things," the judge responded. "But the conduct charged was of such a bad nature that it offsets the good."

Questions remained about the raid to catch the man called "one of the world's most dangerous narcotics kingpins." Many in Tivoli Gardens were angry about the siege. Was so much force justified, they asked, even to capture a man as notorious as Coke, when it put innocent lives in danger? Who was to blame—the police and army, or Coke himself, for using Tivoli and its people to barricade himself from arrest? Many demanded an investigation, so soldiers would be held responsible for their actions. But some Jamaicans believed a crackdown was the only way. "Tivoli Gardens is one of the worst places in Jamaica," one woman told reporters, "and it is time something is done about that community. It is like a kingdom within an island." The neighborhood is still healing from the assault, and it continues to be a place where many struggle to get by.

Others find reasons to hope, cautiously, that Coke's downfall will signal a new beginning for a troubled place. One Jamaican reporter wrote about his wish that Coke would now "sing his heart out"—naming those who helped him run his criminal empire—and root out corruption in Jamaica. "The Coke empire has crumbled," wrote another. "Time will tell if it will be buried forever."

OSAMA BIN LADEN: NIGHT RAID ON A TERRORIST

NAME: Osama bin Laden

BORN: March 10, 1957, in Riyadh, Saudi Arabia

WANTED FOR: Leading a terrorist organization in attacks against the United States, including the September 11, 2001, attacks, which killed 3,000 people

LOCATION OF CHASE: global, but focused on Afghanistan and Pakistan

DURATION: 13 years (1998–May 2, 2011)

LAW ENFORCEMENT INVOLVED: U.S. military intelligence; CIA; Special Operations Forces, including Navy SEALs

Afghanistan, 2011

On a cloudless May night, a team of Navy SEALs received the orders they had been waiting for. Operation Neptune Spear was a "go." Twenty-three men clambered into two Black Hawk helicopters on an airfield in Jalalabad, Afghanistan. Both helicopters were equipped with stealth features that hid them from radar and muffled their noise. Soon they would fly east, secretly cross the Pakistan border, and head for a target north of the capital: a house in a large compound, surrounded by high concrete walls.

Crouched next to the SEALs on the helicopter floor was a Pakistani interpreter and a combat assault dog called Cairo. The interpreter would fend off any curious locals who interrupted the raid; the dog could sniff out anyone hidden in a secret vault. The SEALs had rehearsed for this moment in the desert of Nevada. Storming a replica of the house and compound, they honed their assault plan: the first helicopter would hover over the compound and drop ropes; a dozen men would then climb down into the yard. The second helicopter would land briefly and let out the interpreter, dog, and four SEALs. They would patrol the perimeter and make sure the mission unfolded without intrusion. The second helicopter would then hover over the main building, allowing seven more SEALs to "fast-rope" down to the roof.

The target of Neptune Spear, if intelligence proved correct, would be located on the third floor of the main house: Osama bin Laden, leader of the terrorist group al Qaeda, whose militants had carried out the September 11, 2001, attacks on the United States.

NAVY SEALS

Part of the U.S. Navy, the SEALs (short for Sea Air and Land) are a special operations force trained to undertake reconnaissance missions and small-scale raids or assaults on enemy targets. Members of the Navy who want to join the SEALs undergo several months of challenging training, both on land and underwater, where combat and demolitions are practiced. The mission name "Neptune Spear" was chosen because of the trident of Neptune, Roman god of the sea, worn on the badge of every SEAL who succeeds in passing the grueling training.

Neptune Spear was a small force, but they hoped that would work to their advantage. They would have stealth and surprise on their side. Once the Black Hawks had passed into Pakistani air space, four Chinook helicopters—much larger transport aircraft—took off from Jalalabad to follow them. Two landed within Afghanistan's border, while the other two flew to a desolate valley inside Pakistan, about 15 minutes from the target. There the pilots and extra SEALs waited—if something went wrong, the Chinook teams would provide extra fuel or extract the troops. But no one else would be coming to their aid. Secrecy was so key to the mission's success that further support by bombers or fighter planes could not be risked. The Black Hawks themselves flew without lights on the moonless night, the pilots relying on night-vision goggles.

At the same time, 12,000 kilometers (7,500 miles) away in Washington, D.C., President Obama and his security advisers gathered in a small room. By video and audio, they were in contact with the head of the CIA and with Vice Admiral William McRaven in Afghanistan—the commander of the mission. They were about to watch the SEAL operation in real time, as a stealth drone flying over Abbottabad filmed and fed events to a laptop computer. All eyes fixed on the monitors displaying events in grainy black-and-white video.

9/11

On September 11, 2001, al Qaeda militants hijacked four U.S. airplanes, crashing two into the World Trade Center towers in New York City, and one into the Pentagon, headquarters of the U.S. Department of Defense, near Washington, D.C. The fourth plane crashed in the countryside of Pennsylvania after passengers struggled to reclaim control of the plane from the hijackers. Nearly 3,000 people died in the attacks, including hundreds of police officers and firefighters who fought to rescue those trapped in the New York City blaze.

Ever since Tora Bora, the hunt for bin Laden had been frustrated by a lack of reliable information. The CIA's efforts to recruit sources had resulted mostly in hearsay and untrustworthy leads. Bin Laden had discovered ways to hide from the U.S. military's formidable tracking technology. Satellites scanned cell phone calls worldwide for his

OSAMA BIN LADEN

Born in Saudi Arabia, Osama bin Laden founded the terrorist group known as al Qaeda ("the base") while in Afghanistan, and beginning in the 1990s declared his intention of waging a war against the United States. Under his leadership, al Qaeda trained and funded terrorists to attack U.S. targets, including embassies and the ship USS *Cole*. In Afghanistan, bin Laden was sheltered by the Taliban, the extremist militia governing the country. After the September 11 attacks, the United States led a coalition that overthrew the Taliban, and bin Laden went into hiding. The closest U.S. forces came to catching bin Laden was at his hideout in Tora Bora, a complex of caves among the mountains of southeastern Afghanistan. In December 2001, a combination of air strikes and ground forces failed to dislodge bin Laden, who broadcast a defiant message by radio afterward. The U.S. eventually offered a $25 million reward for information leading to his capture, but bin Laden remained elusive for the next nine years.

"voice print," which the U.S. had on file. But bin Laden stopped communicating by phone. Instead, he had face-to-face conversations with trusted couriers, who relayed instructions to followers. The breakthrough in the search came with the discovery of one such courier. They tracked his movements through Pakistani informants, who told the CIA they had seen the courier driving his white Suzuki jeep to a complex in Abbottabad.

The walled compound, about an acre in size, was located in a prosperous suburb, about a kilometer (half-mile) away from a Pakistani military academy, which made it seem like a strange hiding place. Through local informants, CIA agents pieced together the pattern of activities of those who lived in the compound. As many as 20 people, including women and children, lived inside. Could bin Laden be living there with his wives and children? Spying on the compound proved very difficult. It had no telephone lines or Internet. Orbiting satellites could capture images inside the high walls, but no clear picture of bin Laden emerged. A man took a walk in the vegetable garden each day—like someone getting exercise in a prison yard. But a tarpaulin had been hung overhead, preventing an accurate satellite image. CIA analysts called the walking man "the pacer." Whoever lived there was clearly hiding. But was the pacer bin Laden?

The CIA's level of confidence that bin Laden was there ranged from 60 to 90 percent.

All the evidence was circumstantial, but it was the best lead on his whereabouts since Tora Bora, over nine years earlier. Two questions remained: first, should they act on what was only a strong possibility that bin Laden was there? And, second, what action should they take?

The compound was surrounded by blast-proof walls that would protect those inside from small-scale attacks. Dropping a large-scale bomb on the whole compound was ruled out: it would devastate the area, killing innocent people and the children known to be in the compound, as well as angering the Pakistani government. It would also destroy traces of the occupants, including proof that bin Laden had been there. Some favored a small, secretive raid. Satellite imagery had provided a rough map of the compound's interior buildings—enough to plan a commando attack. If it turned out that bin Laden was not there, the team could withdraw quickly and keep the failed operation covert. Plans for a raid had to be kept absolutely secret, even from the Pakistani government. While Pakistan was officially an ally in catching al Qaeda fugitives, the U.S. suspected its intelligence agency continued to share information with the Taliban. The risk of a warning leaking out to bin Laden was too great. That left the thorny issue of conducting a raid inside Pakistan without its government's knowledge—an act sure to strain Pakistan's relations with the U.S. But the overriding goal of getting bin Laden prevailed. President Obama approved preparations for the raid.

The Black Hawks' flight to Abbottabad, where the compound was located, would take 90 minutes. Once there, SEALs

 were to complete their mission within 30 minutes. Since the decision had been made not to involve local Pakistani forces, the whole raid and withdrawal must be completed before local military became alarmed and investigated. Command hoped that if any locals heard the sound of helicopters, they would assume the aircraft were heading for the local military academy. As the low-flying Black Hawks sped closer to Abbottabad from the northwest, the SEALs prepared for the descent, checking their weapons, securing their helmets, and pulling down their night-vision goggles in the moments before the side door gaped open.

The helicopters were over their target by 12:30 a.m. As planned, the first helicopter descended to hover over the compound yard. The pilot quickly sensed something was wrong: the helicopter began to drop much too fast. It was, as pilots say, "settling with power." The compound's high concrete walls, the hot night air, and the extra weight of the helicopter's stealth technology all contributed to a dangerous vortex sucking the aircraft down. The helicopter's tail hit the compound wall; the pilot knew he had lost control. His fast-thinking response was to deliberately push the nose of his aircraft into the soft earth of the garden. His quick reaction saved himself and the SEALs on board.

In Washington, the men and women watching the video feed held their breath. Minutes passed. Over the secure line, the voice of Admiral McRaven in Afghanistan broke the room's silence: "We will now be amending the mission. . . . My men are prepared for this contingency and they will deal with it." The mission would continue; the Chinook pilots were radioed that their backup would be needed when the time came to get out.

The pilot of the second helicopter had witnessed it all, and decided not to risk hovering over the compound as planned. He brought his aircraft down outside the walls.

After making sure no one was injured in the crash, the dozen

SEALs in the first helicopter dropped out the open door. They ran toward an inner wall, each encumbered with nearly 30 kilograms (66 pounds) of gear, their goggles casting everything around them in shades of green. The demolitions team set charges on the hinges of the wall's iron gate, which fell over with a loud explosion. The team streamed down an alleyway between two high walls, blew another gate open, and found themselves in an inner courtyard.

Meanwhile, the SEALs from the second helicopter had adapted quickly to the change in plan. Those assigned to patrol the perimeter were already in place. The rest headed for a gate on the north side of the compound—the Plan B entry point. After blowing it open with explosives, they were dismayed to find a brick wall blocking the way. They dashed to the next northern gate, radioing the SEALs already inside to let them in.

The helicopter crash had destroyed the advantage of surprise. Every moment counted now; it was essential to move faster than those who had been awakened and were beginning to react. The SEALs broke into three-man teams to cover the area. They expected to encounter up to five armed men in the compound, including the courier, his brother, and bin Laden's adult sons. Inside the buildings, rooms had to be checked and cleared of booby traps—unlikely considering families appeared to live there, but still possible. Nearing the guesthouse, they were met with loud gunshots through the closed door. Since their own weapons had silencers, they knew it was an enemy gunman. The SEALs returned fire.

No more than 10 minutes after the helicopter crashed, the first SEALs entered the main house. From this point events unfolded rapidly and in the dark—CIA agents had cut off electricity to the area. The overhead drone could not film what happened inside. What is known is based on the memories of those who took part, accounts that sometimes conflict.

Military intelligence had guessed that bin Laden lived on the top two floors with his family. Bin Laden's bedroom was thought to be on the third floor, but no one had definite knowledge of the layout inside. As the first team swept through the pitch-dark ground floor, they shot the courier's brother as he emerged with a gun from a bedroom.

The foot of the staircase to the next floor was blocked by a metal gate. Again the SEALs blew it open with explosives. Moving quietly up the narrow spiraling staircase, they encountered and shot an armed man, who turned out to be one of bin Laden's sons. They proceeded upstairs to the third, and last, floor. The house was now deadly quiet, their footsteps the only sound. Whoever was up there was waiting silently.

The staircase landing led into a narrow hall, with a door on each side. A tall man with a bearded face was spotted retreating into one of the bedrooms. It was bin Laden. The SEALs in the lead followed, and were suddenly barred by a woman who advanced on them, shouting. The first SEAL through the door—concerned she might be bearing explosives—grabbed her and moved her quickly to a corner of the room to save his comrades from any blast. Within moments, bin Laden was shot dead by the SEAL team.

The team relayed the code word for success to their commander, McRaven: "Geronimo." But McRaven wanted to be sure—had their quarry been captured or killed?

"Is he EKIA [Enemy Killed In Action]?" McRaven radioed back.

Seconds passed. "Roger, Geronimo EKIA," the voice of a SEAL replied. McRaven passed the message on to those listening in Washington. The SEALs snapped photos of the dead man's face to be sent to Washington for identification. A medic took DNA samples from the body.

In the minutes that followed, SEALs gathered computers, disks, flash drives, and cell phones— capturing information on al Qaeda's plans was also part of the mission. Outside, the interpreter warded off worried locals who had gathered after hearing the helicopters. "A security operation is underway," he told them, "Go

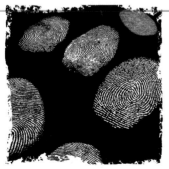

home." With luck they would assume the soldiers inside were local forces.

Before leaving, the SEALs set the crashed helicopter with explosives. They must not leave it behind in usable condition, and its instrument panel and radio posed a security risk. They herded the women and children in the compound to a safe point away from the helicopter. The SEALs set the charges on a five-minute timer before half the men climbed into the second Black Hawk and took off. Moments later the Chinook landed to bear the remaining team away.

They had spent 38 minutes in the compound—8 minutes longer than planned. After an emergency refueling stop, the helicopters returned to Jalalabad air base, bringing the body believed to be Osama bin Laden. McRaven met the helicopters as they landed, impatient to identify the body beyond any doubt. Bin Laden was known to be almost 2 meters (6 feet 4 inches) tall, but no one had a tape measure.

"You," said McRaven to a SEAL who was roughly that height. "Lie down next to him." The heights matched. That night the U.S. military contacted Pakistan's chief of army staff to inform him about the raid. Days later al Qaeda confirmed the death of their leader, and pledged revenge.

When Admiral McRaven met President Obama at the White House, Obama handed the admiral a tape measure. The president also met with the SEAL team and pilots. He was surprised to learn a dog had been on the mission.

"I'd like to meet that dog," he said.

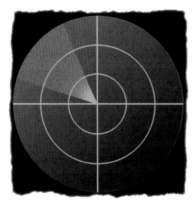

"If you want to meet the dog, Mr. President," the squadron commander smiled, "I advise you to bring treats." For a moment at least, the joke broke the tension of so grim a mission.

The American hunt for Osama bin Laden had lasted 13 years— ever since the CIA first hatched plans to capture the terrorist leader in 1998. For the United States, it was a long-awaited success in a search that had begun to look hopeless. The mayor of New York City hoped the news would bring comfort and closure to all those who lost loved ones in the September 11 attacks. Although the death of bin Laden did not guarantee an end to al Qaeda terrorism, President Obama called it America's most significant achievement to date in the effort to defeat al Qaeda.

In the hours after the mission, U.S. officials debated what to do with the terrorist's remains. A burial at sea was chosen. As in the case of Adolf Eichmann, no grave would be left to become a shrine for extremist followers. Within a day of Operation Neptune Spear, the body of Osama bin Laden was flown to a U.S aircraft carrier in the Arabian Sea. After the rites of Muslim burial were observed, it was weighted and slipped into the water.

CHASING CRIMINALS TODAY

As these eight stories have shown, methods for hunting criminals have evolved over time. And right now, searches are underway around the world. Is there a typical method for chasing criminals in the 21st century? Rather than calling a hundred police officers together for a briefing, a modern search more likely enlists police forces across large areas through good communication. Typically, police enter a "wanted" suspect's information into an electronic database. When officers in one city enter a name or license plate number into a police computer, they see at once if the person is being pursued by another police force. Any instructions to detain the suspect are also displayed. In Canada, this national database is managed by the RCMP, while in the United States, the FBI provides a similar electronic resource. When a suspect becomes the target of a national search, a package is distributed to officers across the country, including photos and identifying features. And if the hunt becomes global, police cooperate through Interpol.

Police can use surveillance to catch their suspect—watching from a vehicle or a helicopter. But more invasive methods, such as eavesdropping on telephone conversations with a wiretap, usually require a warrant from a judge. Police also recognize the value of tips from the public. The FBI's "Ten Most Wanted Fugitives" program, which uses newspapers, TV, and radio to publicize a suspect's name and picture, has led to hundreds of arrests since it was started in 1950. The listed fugitives are wanted for crimes ranging from armed robbery to prison escapes to fraud. In one of the shortest hunts, a suspect was arrested within two hours of making the Most Wanted list. But not every chase has led to a capture: one of the longest-sought fugitives has been on the list for 30 years.

Modern criminal hunts involve teamwork among many kinds of crime experts. Besides those out combing terrain for the fugitive are all the people working behind the scenes: researchers who find clues in the mountains of case documents, criminal profilers who come up with a likely description and potential behavior of a still unknown suspect, crime-scene experts who conduct scientific analysis of physical evidence. This complex teamwork seems a long way from the posse of local constables and volunteers in past searches. Yet the goal is still the same—to bring a criminal to justice, no matter how tough the chase.

MAIN SOURCES

Aharoni, Zvi, and Wilhelm Dietl. Translated by Helmut Bögler. *Operation Eichmann: The Truth About the Pursuit, Capture and Trial.* New York: John Wiley & Sons, 1997.

Bergen, Peter L. *Manhunt: The Ten-Year Search for Bin Laden from 9/11 to Abbottabad.* Toronto: Doubleday Canada, 2012.

Bowden, Mark. *The Finish: The Killing of Osama Bin Laden.* New York: Atlantic Monthly Press, 2012.

Brenner, Susan W. *Cybercrime: Criminal Threats from Cyberspace.* Santa Barbara, California: Praeger, 2010.

"Famous Cases and Criminals: Aldrich Ames." www.fbi.gov/about-us/history/famous-cases/aldrich-hazen-ames.

"Famous Cases and Criminals: John Dillinger." www.fbi.gov/about-us/history/famous-cases/john-dillinger.

Gorn, Elliott J. *Dillinger's Wild Ride: The Year that Made America's Public Enemy Number One.* New York: Oxford University Press, 2009.

Gow, David, and Richard Norton-Taylor. "Surfing Superhighwaymen." *The Guardian.* December 7, 1996.

Grimes, Sandra, and Jeanne Vertefeuille. *Circle of Treason: A C.I.A. Account of Traitor Aldrich Ames and the Men He Betrayed.* Annapolis, Maryland: Naval Institute Press, 2012.

Harel, Isser. *The House on Garibaldi Street.* New York: Frank Cass & Co., 1997.

Lacey, Marc, and Kareem Fahim. "Disguises May Have Helped Jamaican Drug Lord Elude Arrest." *New York Times.* June 23, 2010.

McIntosh, Neil. *Cyber Crime.* Chicago: Raintree, 2003.

North, Dick. *The Mad Trapper of Rat River: A True Story of Canada's Biggest Manhunt.* Guilford, Connecticut: The Lyons Press, 2005.

"Notable Hacks." www.pbs.org/wgbh/pages/frontline/shows/hackers /whoare/notable.html.

Rohter, Larry. "The Noriega Case." *New York Times.* January 6, 1990.

Runkle, Benjamin. *Wanted Dead or Alive: Manhunts from Geronimo to Bin Laden.* New York: Palgrave Macmillan, 2011.

Schmidle, Nicholas, "Getting Bin Laden." *New Yorker.* August 8, 2011.

Schwartz, Mattathias. "As Jamaican Drug Lord Is Sentenced, U.S. Still Silent on Massacre." *newyorker.com.* June 8, 2012.

Schwartz, Mattathias, "A Massacre in Jamaica." *The New Yorker.* December 12, 2011.

Smith, Barbara. *The Mad Trapper: Unearthing a Mystery.* Surrey, British Columbia: Heritage House Publishing Co., 2009.

Spaulding, Gary. "The Rise and Fall of the Coke Empire." *Jamaica Gleaner.* June 5, 2010.

"We Hope that Mr. Christopher Coke Will Sing His Heart Out." Editorial. *Jamaica Observer.* September 1, 2011.

Wilson, Nadine. "Blair: I Met with Coke." *Jamaica Observer.* May 31, 2010.

Wise, David. *Nightmover: How Aldrich Ames Sold the CIA to the KGB for $4.6 Million.* New York: Harper Collins, 1995.

INDEX

When is it okay to rebel against authority or break the law? In this thought-provoking book, Laura Scandiffio presents the inspiring stories of eight people whose response to oppression was standing up to defend their rights and the rights of others.

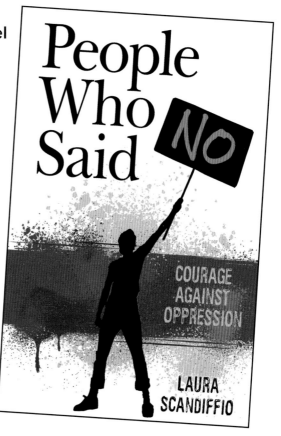

"These inspiring stories of people who challenged the status quo make for riveting reading, as well as excellent starting points for research and discussions about civil disobedience, ethics, and morality."
—*Kirkus Reviews*

"... reads like good historical fiction."
—*School Library Journal*

"Themes described here are universal ... with highly engaging and up-to-date exemplars of the right ways to say no."
—*Booklist*

"This superb book should be on every library shelf and should be mandatory reading for high school students."
—*ForeWord Reviews*